THE STRUGGLE
OF THE JUGGLE

THE STRUGGLE OF THE JUGGLE

By Kelly Rice

The Struggle of the Juggle

ISBN: 9798699246007

Cover design by Sooraj Mathew

Edited by Hilary Jastram & Kathryn DeHoyos

Graphics: Flat Icons/photo3idea_studio

 BOOKMARK

<u>DEDICATION</u>

This book is dedicated to my wonderful support system. It is not one person but a group who have inspired me. First and foremost, my husband, whose unwavering support has allowed me to spread my wings and achieve goals well beyond my wildest dreams. Because of his understanding of my desires and his unconditional love, I am here today writing this book. You are my best friend, and I am eternally grateful for your encouragement. And my children, for their patience and understanding as their momma focused on accomplishing her life goals, and whose endless love supported me along the way.

To them and to all of you who have wiped away my tears throughout this journey, thank you. Thank you to those who keep me motivated daily—too many of you to list. To all the haters who have pushed me in ways no one else could, I thank you, too!

Next, to the women who inspired me to press on despite how challenging life was, for the long phone calls when I felt like giving up and the encouragement you have given me to forge ahead, I thank you—again, too many of you to list; these are my co-workers and my network of hard-working moms juggling their own life goals every single day. Thank you for being there. Mandy, you will always be the one I call to celebrate my successes with; you have seen me at my worst and have helped me to become the best damn version of myself that I can be. I would be absolutely lost without you. I am so glad that you talked me out of my self-doubt.

To my brother, who, despite how often I get caught up in life and work, never shames me for forgetting to text him back, you will always remain my like-minded rock. You always "get me" without explanation or judgment. You are an avid supporter of all the things that I do, and you encourage me every step of the way. Thank you for your endless love.

TABLE OF CONTENTS

FOREWORD

Fresh out of college with an English Literature degree, I found that no distinct jobs existed for me unless I had a teaching certificate, so I started asking close friends for job connections.

My best friend's brother arranged an interview for me for a position as a mortgage account executive (AE) for a small, family-owned, private lending corporation. And before I knew it, I was on the frontline, selling our mortgage financing products to brokerage firms with zero knowledge for how the loans worked or what most of the financing terminology meant in the broader scheme of things.

As an AE, I was assigned a processor to handle the loan paperwork and get the loans to fund. I had no idea who this Kelly Rice was, firing off her emails from her ivory tower, but I was going to find out!

Due to my complete lack of knowledge, I became incredibly defensive, and the fact that I was not making much money did not help.

One day, Kelly called me to go over my loan pipeline, and I had to ask, "what?" a couple of times because she talked so fast with way more knowledge than me.

Personally, feeling the stress grow as her updates all sounded like bad news, I had the nerve to take an attitude with her.

Let's just say that disrespect was not the well-chosen tool for this duel.

Before I knew what was happening, there was Kelly Rice standing directly in front of me. The very first thought to cross my mind at that childish age of twenty-three was, *I am gonna lose IF we start boxing.*

Here I was starting a new relationship with the intention to dominate when I had never even met Kelly, nor had I really given her a chance! I was definitely out of line, and she made sure to let me know,

"I don't think we've met, and I'm also not sure who you think you are, but nobody talks to me that way;

especially you."

Wow!

Granted, I earned every word that came out of her mouth, and my now nervous expression owned it. "I'm sorry for disrespecting you. Let's start over. I'm Kristy; nice to meet you. I'm looking forward to working with you."

I had never liked people who spoke with a certain degree of authority over any situation involving me, and I was going to come to realize that not only would Kelly go on to mentor me in my mortgage endeavors, but she would also teach me about true friendship.

From that day, we began to talk more and more until we were having lunch together or hanging out at my house after work before she drove her second hour home.

Together, we learned what we didn't know, and we problem-solved with one another to get the loans closed. I was fortunate enough to work at the next company with Kelly because I gave her the information she needed to get the job. I never once doubted her tenacity or her ability to perform, nor did I ever feel threatened by her in a competitive way.

We both were now underwriting processors, and we were so on fire with the passion to know more, but most importantly, to deliver to the customer.

I began to really see who Kelly was, and I became inspired by the fact that she drove so far for a better opportunity and that every sacrifice she made was for everyone but herself.

She would often spend the entire last week of each month not seeing her husband and children much, but rather, commuting two hours each direction and staying at work for well over twelve hours per shift.

Let me make one thing clear: the people who did what we did rarely gave themselves to the work as Kelly did.

Very few people come close to the winner Kelly Rice proved to be time and time again.

Do not misconstrue my use of the term "winner," as nothing ever seemed to come easy for her, but that never scared her because it takes failures and losses to reach wins.

Plus, what else could scare you when you were riding the overdraft wave at the bank? The years we spent together were the most formative years of my life because I learned how to truly care about what happens to other people even if I do not know them, and I learned how to persevere even in times of struggle and adversity because of her.

<u>INTRODUCTION</u>

Have you ever felt like you are not in control of your life?

My life has been a collection of these moments, which have paved the path of my future.

Using the stones I have tripped over as a reminder and carrying the surface scars life has left me, I will share with you my tale of powerful perseverance.

Change your mindset, and you will change your life. We are not victims of life's circumstance; we are living the consequence of actions. Not all of our actions are meant to be rewarding. Some are meant to teach us a lesson.

Hitting rock bottom is where all of pain is felt, and the reward is just out of reach. We have all been there; we just need to choose not to torture ourselves by staying on the bottom. We are not meant to live there; we are meant to reflect on these moments, reassess our priorities, and develop a plan of action.

Do you think you are losing your mind with your children? You are and so have the rest of us.

Here is the beauty in raising tiny humans; they teach us just as much as we teach them. We learn to be compassionate on a level that we never truly understood before having children. We learn how to give and receive unconditional love. These babies help keep us motivated each and every day. They give us the courage to push forward when life proves difficult.

Let's face it; it is kind of hard to lie in bed all day feeling sorry for ourselves when we are desperately needed for our children's survival.

As your children grow older, life becomes less chaotic and allows us the chance to be even more dedicated to our careers and aspirations. But it can also be a time when we feel the pain of being less needed by our families. For me, this was the time to invest in myself.

I used to think that I was being selfish if I took that time away from my kids, but now that they are grown, I can promise you that they truly have become exactly as my husband and I have taught them. My working had no effect on them, and they became my cheerleaders. In hindsight, I wish I would have allowed myself the peace of mind knowing how they would turn out.

It may not be too late for you, so I urge you to reconsider your mom guilt.

Your kids are just fine.

CHAPTER 1

NEVER LET YOUR FAILURE DEFINE YOUR FUTURE

"Failure is not the end. It is the setback before defeat." ~Katherine Divolis

Staring at the empty refrigerator again, wondering how I'd let my life derail, I tried to scrape together something to eat for dinner with nothing to choose from, aside from condiments and essentials.

The days of having the luxury of food choices were long gone and in the same breath, so was I. The sun was starting to set out the kitchen window, and it served as a reminder that this was my reality; it was time to pull off another dinner creation out of nothing.

I could no longer recognize the woman I was.

I had become someone other than myself—someone who had given up, someone who had decided to accept the criticism of others as truth.

I had succumbed to failure and accepted it as my reality.

In that moment, staring at those empty shelves, I felt as if I were an outsider in my own life. I was incapable of taking care of my kids and had lost the optimistic entrepreneurial spirit that had once inspired me.

These were the days when it was a struggle to think that everything would be okay.

When things got really hopeless, I took comfort in my safe zone. My husband. Although he assured me everything would be okay, I couldn't see it.

Time seemed to move rapidly after the mortgage meltdown, and my savings account depleted at the same rate. I had to find a new job and fast. One thing I did know was that I would avoid the field where I had just been terminated.

How could I return to work in the same industry that had built me up, only to tear me right back down? How could I find comfort in an industry that was crumbling? So many talented people were now competing and fighting for the remaining positions available.

It was a time when foreclosures plagued hard-working homeowners. A time when everything I had worked so hard to master seemed unnecessary. My time spent away from my children—for what?

I trusted that none of the job openings would last long. It would take years to bounce back from the economic crisis we were now facing, and so, I told myself that I would not return to the industry until it was stable again.

I was no longer carefree and loving. Instead, I had allowed myself to be consumed by despair and to wallow in self-pity. Life and the consequences of actions can bring you to your knees.

I went from having it all—a career that I absolutely loved, two kids, financial freedom, a husband that I adored, and a pretty little house on a corner lot—to losing everything that I had worked so hard for.

I was, at my peak, living my dream and proud of where I had come from. The hard work that I'd put into mastering the craft of mortgages and the time spent away from my family had all been for a good cause— because I was giving my children a good life. And I know that money isn't everything, but it is necessary.

I had been a part of the industry that left so many hurting and losing their homes. Indirectly or not, it was a reality that rocked me to my core and left me shaken, unlike anything I have ever felt.

Every night when I tucked myself into bed, I would count my pennies in my head as I tried to sleep, determined to find a way to make every single utility stay on, and keep a roof over our heads. In the dim light, I would stare at the mirrored reflection of myself, bouncing off the closet doors, unrecognizable to myself, before allowing my eyes to shut in hopes of sleep.

Then I would panic, and my eyes would snap open again.

Fear shook my body, and my stomach would tie in knots. I no longer dreamed of what could be, but rather how ashamed I was of myself for letting my family down.

I wasn't a dreamer; I was a failure.

I ran through every hurtful word ever spoken to me, over and over again, until it cemented my worthlessness. I used the criticism as a means to berate myself, which only made me sink further and further into a depression. I felt useless, and I was going to make sure that I reminded myself of it.

Looking back, I now understand that part of any journey must be accompanied by failure, but my life had taken a desperate turn. It wasn't even a turn, but more like a plunge off a cliff without a parachute.

I had fallen so deep I had no idea how to pull myself out.

Losing my job as a loan specialist was hard but watching the entire industry crumble before my eyes was sickening.

I was unsure which bank to even call to secure a job because they were all being shut down. As it turns out, extending credit to everyone wasn't ideal. Banks were loaning money to everyone because there was an appetite for the sale of them. Was it right? No, but that didn't stop it from happening, and this went on for a very long time. At some point, that bubble burst, leaving every position in my entire professional sphere in jeopardy.

The mortgage industry had become too volatile.

There was no more security in the field that I loved so much.

I can never explain the feelings I had or the guilt that I struggled with when this happened.

My boys were very young at the time and were excited to have their momma back home. I think in their heads, a job loss meant bath time with their mom, who had been missing as she worked so late the last few years.

But this was hardly the case because I wasn't truly there. I was lost in my head and was not okay. Instead of them finding the carefree mother they needed, they found a sad, silent one—which wasn't fair to them.

Their father, who remained steadfast in his support, did all he could to help pull me away from my thoughts.

Still, his belief in me didn't change what I thought of myself. His desperate pleas for me to cheer up, fell upon deaf ears.

I was a homeowner with two car payments and two young boys. I had not a clue what to do with myself, but I will tell you what I wanted to do. I wanted to sleep and cry.

Nothing would ever be the same.

At this point, I was unsure what exactly would be the outcome of the field that I had just spent years training myself in. It was as if I were watching a slow train derail. Everyone in the industry knew that the collapse was coming, but no matter how hard we tried, we couldn't plan for the outcome.

Prior to the great mortgage meltdown, I spent many late nights lying wide awake with anxiety. It was inevitable, and I didn't have time to prepare for it. I was young and spent every hard dollar I had earned. We had no savings account, just large payments. It was enough to give anyone anxiety.

Before I was let go, the environment was stressful. By day my co-workers and I had been led into meetings, being reassured that our jobs were safe and that nothing was going to change. It was business as usual. But I know now those were empty promises made to prevent panic. It was a lie of the worst magnitude—one that affected the employees that our employers claimed to care about so passionately.

I may not be perfect, but I would never lead a team into chaos without setting a clear expectation of what was to come.

The silver lining was that I used my work's missteps as an opportunity to learn a great deal about how to handle delicate situations with employees.

I vowed to be a better leader for my team than the people who came before me if ever my chance to lead was given.

The damage done to the market when the housing bubble popped was felt across the entire industry. And it all led to the single hardest moment in my lifetime.

For two years after the crash, I did whatever work I could from home, working for anyone who would pay me. It was so good to be with my kids, but difficult to see any damn hope since my income was significantly less than our monthly expenses.

I simply could not make ends meet, and my life went into a downward spiral that I could not control.

I had become a master of hanging on. Paying one bill and letting another one slide. My home was worth less than what I owed on it, thanks to the declining home market, and I could not get out from under it. My payment was outrageous because I not only had one mortgage; I also had a second mortgage. I couldn't reduce my payments on that either, because I'd lost my job before the market really suffered any losses. The programs to mitigate foreclosure didn't materialize until well after I fell upon trouble.

As a bonus, the result of me asking for help led my mortgage company to tack on tens of thousands of dollars yet again to my mortgage. That meant I was now paying an insane monthly payment on a home that would never appraise for enough to make sense of those two mortgages. But I would not be alone in this occurrence; many others would soon be in the same gut-wrenching situation.

Imagine that.

I was in the field of helping others buy homes, and I couldn't manage the payments on my own home.

I was skipping one payment to make another. The agony just wouldn't end. I had already lost my career, home, and pride, and now, I was struggling to keep our vehicles while keeping a roof over our heads and the heat on. I clipped coupons until I reduced my grocery bill to next to nothing because that is what we had to live on—nothing.

But it wasn't enough. As my frustration grew, my liveliness left. Agony is best described as extreme suffering, and I was not just enduring mental suffering; I was also suffering physically.

I was inches from losing it all.

The pain felt while watching everything that I'd worked so hard for being ripped away made me want to vomit. I went from having a stable environment for my kids to losing the very home in which we were raising them. The options at the time when I started to default on my mortgage were limited.

I could sell my home, but if I did that, I would need to sell assets I didn't have to get out from underneath. It simply wasn't worth the mortgage I owed, and I had no savings accounts or 401k from which to pull the money needed to make up the losses. I couldn't get a cheaper payment and could only see one way out.

I could face the humiliation of a foreclosure.

That devastated me.

By this point, my credit was absolutely ruined.

And just like my pride, I didn't have a lick of savings left.

So we faced the music and a foreclosure.

Eventually, we had to move my kids out of the home that we all loved. We found a cheaper place to call home and tried to make our children as comfortable as possible. A tough conversation with them about leaving a home they loved was muted by welcoming new neighbors, and I was so very thankful for that. It was a pause from the pain of me explaining how I had failed, and it gave me time to regain my composure so I could go through the motions of moving into a house that wasn't our home.

The one thing I had always been able to rely on throughout my life was finding a job. I had been working since the age of thirteen.

Needing to find a job this time was no different. I needed employment that was outside of my comfort zone.

I did want to learn about insurance, so I figured there was no better way to understand a necessity in life than to take a job where I would be assisting customers with benefit explanations all day long. And that is exactly what I did! Granted, it was not my preferred position, but it did provide me with a wealth of knowledge about medical insurance that I carried for my family.

Even though I was working, I had taken a $90,000 per year salary cut as I paid for the debts that originated when I had an entirely different income. Convinced I was never going to return to an industry that had taken my life and career away, I settled for a job that included midnights and insane overtime to help me offset some of the financial burden I faced. The tradeoff was that I could work from home and be with my children, but that benefit came with a price. That price left me feeling empty in every way, including in my wallet.

In this new position, I worked about sixty-five hours a week from home while I snatched up any overtime I could. Overtime wasn't for fun money; it was damage control, and I couldn't work enough to pay off everything.

My one job was to provide for my children and to encourage them. It was to lead by example. But I couldn't help but wonder what kind of example I was setting by allowing myself to be in such a challenging financial position.

My children were not proud of me. They wondered why we had no food in our house and looked to me to find a solution. Being strapped down with only one income was not something anyone wanted to have a conversation about with their child, most certainly, not when you feel the blame of the income loss. I was now a mother and wife who stopped wanting to put on makeup or even get dressed. Working from home made me a prisoner of the walls. Instead of reminding myself of who I really was, I simply gave up.

At the same time, I didn't want to compromise being close to home and missing my kids again. Besides, I had convinced myself that if I went back into the mortgage industry, it would only lead to agony.

The truth is, this event in my life made my kids both humble and appreciative of what we had all gone through as a family. Yes, I had worries about not being able to provide for them, but kids are resilient. My boys were fine.

As I thought about what I would do, I realized I couldn't use them as an excuse anymore.

In reality, I figured out that I didn't want to go back into the mortgage industry because I didn't want to experience the rejection and risk again. So, I used my kids as an excuse to stay safe and complacent.

It wasn't a matter of just getting back at it either. I was shaken over what had happened and losing so much.

I needed to heal from what I had endured, and that didn't happen overnight.

No, it took me three long years to love myself and have faith in my abilities again. It wasn't that I was at fault for the entire mortgage collapse and losing my job that held me back; it was how I tore myself apart and assumed responsibility for the damage that was outside of my control.

Misplaced accountability resulted in extremely toxic self-abuse. I had to find a way over that hurdle. I had to find my strength and confidence again, and I didn't know how to do that. Loving yourself despite your faults is not something that is taught.

If I had never gone through what I did, I wouldn't be who I am today. That's why I am not sad when I look back at these times; I am empowered by them.

I continued down the path of "why me" for a bit longer, clipping my coupons, and being angry at the world.

When my kid wanted to play football, I couldn't afford it and had to ask for his fees that year to be waived. As I stood there in complete humiliation in front of the coach, I cautiously looked around to see if anyone was noticing me talk about how poor we really were. As horrible as it felt, I was ashamed but still not rattled enough to take control of my future. It was just another thing to cry over at night.

My thought process was clouded by doubt, but it was evolving with time. Even though I wrestled with the urge to stay in bed, I pushed on. I needed to see that we lead our lives based on the value of our worth, and I wasn't quite there yet. I was still learning about myself, and I was still a really young mother who felt defeated. Because of this, I spent a great deal of time trying to figure out how to look myself in the eye without running away from my image in the mirror.

It took me a long time to realize that you will fail time and time again, but failure is crucial to your growth as a mother or professional. You must understand why you failed so that you can make adjustments in the future. We make decisions every single day, and they will not always be the right ones. But when that happens, you will stand back up again, this time more resilient, better prepared, and wiser.

Just like the turn of a doorknob, being resilient clicks, and then you begin to understand that it is okay to make mistakes, and it is okay to fail.

Mistakes teach us important life lessons.

Every error in judgment along the way builds us up and gives us a better shot at getting it right.

Every single one of my failures, especially finding myself without a career, helped pave the way to my success. It inspired me to get up, dust myself off, and fight again.

What I learned and what I want to share with you is to have faith in your abilities.

Never give up. You are worth it, and so was I. It just took me a while to remember that. When I finally did, I hit the ground running and never looked back.

Remember, there is no specific deadline for finding yourself after losing your career. It takes extreme courage to discover and believe your worth, and sometimes it takes a bit longer than you might anticipate to get there.

But that's the thing.

It doesn't matter how long it takes for you to recover. Even when it sometimes feels as if you will never find yourself again, I promise you; you will.

Be patient with yourself.

Your feelings are valid.

PART 1:

BEFORE THE CRASH

CHAPTER 2

THE BEAUTY OF FAILURE

"Success is most often achieved by those who don't know that failure is inevitable."
~Coco Chanel

I was fresh out of high school and had absolutely no clue what I wanted to do with my life.

This was complicated by the fact that I fell in love early and moved out shortly after graduation.

I didn't want anything to do with my parent's home and their rules. I was a rebellious teenager and longed to live my way. I could not be there one second longer because I was so eager to start my life. So much so that I rented the first apartment I looked at. I didn't care where my boyfriend, now husband, and I lived, as long as I was out of my parents' home and officially on my own, but I still wanted to be close enough to remain a part of my young brothers' lives.

Growing up, I had a very normal life.

It wasn't that my family hurt me in any way.

It was more that we didn't get along.

I was shown love and spoiled rotten. I listened to Nirvana like most unruly teenagers of the 90s. I was simple and didn't prefer glam—still don't. Give me a sweatshirt and a pair of jeans and ditch the glitter and glam, please. I had a mind of my own, and that caused conflict growing up. I didn't conform to what society or my parents wanted me to be.

The older I became, the harder it was to control me. My parents had a very different idea of what they envisioned for my life than I did and were quite vocal about it. They did not like my husband and made it perfectly clear how they felt, but I refused to have anyone dictate who I decided to love. It was not their call, and their opinion was irrelevant.

That doesn't mean their constant disapproval didn't bother me. It still stings to this day, although we have come a long way. But the messages in our words can leave scars, and just because someone is family, it doesn't mean they have a green light to interfere with your happiness—and my father was never shy about expressing his feelings. We have all done things we were less than proud of, and I am sure I hurt them equally.

I have always been headstrong and raising independent children can be difficult. I understand this now that I am a parent of one. My parents grew weary of that, and as a result, we never really connected.

My mother, who had a later-in-life pregnancy, continued to get more and more exhausted as she aged, especially after my twin brothers were born.

I can't imagine how it must have felt starting over with a new baby when her youngest was ten, but I suspect it was hard, especially with two very demanding newborns. It took a toll on her, and she relied on my sister and me more and more to help care for the twins, and we wanted to be there to do that.

People often say that teenagers are difficult and that they come back to love and respect their parents again when they are older. I would say that I was one of those teenagers. I wanted to place blame on how I was raised or what I didn't get. Even though I was complaining about a lie.

As I said, I was spoiled.

Then at the fun age of eighteen, I was ready to face the world and was fearless in my pursuit. I quickly found out that the notions of "I am owed" or "It's not my fault" are excuses that overtake accountability for our actions. Even as a child, I didn't feel entitled to something I hadn't earned. I just simply wanted to live life by my own rules.

We can all sit around and blame others for how our life turned out; we can associate our upbringing as blame for our actions, but that is not how I choose to view life. I want to be responsible for my future. I would rather think about *how am I going to make a difference in my own life?*

When I focused on being in charge of what I needed to do, the results were priceless. I found myself earning my first dollar and framing it, which led me to work even harder in the pursuit of my goals. I may not have led an easy life with poor early decision-making, but I was holding myself accountable for my own desires, wants, needs, and accomplishments even at a young age and I adored that feeling of accomplishment.

When I moved out of the house, the twins were devastated, and that broke my heart.

I did whatever I could to make the transition easier on them and stayed in the same town as my family. I was within walking distance of their school, so they could see me any time they wanted. And they took full advantage of that opportunity. They would walk over after school and spend every weekend with me.

Moving out was painful for me, too, but only because I knew how much those kids needed me. It's funny how life works like that. We may not always get what we want, but somehow we get what we need. My heart kept me close to the very home that I was trying to get away from.

There I was, just a kid with no idea who I really was, already on my own, thinking I had life all figured out.

Wrong.

I had no clue.

But we don't need to have a plan every step of the way.

I know this now.

Because every single step of my life brought me purpose and happiness and kept me moving forward, I learned about my capabilities. If I could go back in time, I would do it all over again without changing a thing. Each and every one of my life experiences made me who I am, and if I were to change any of that, I am not sure if I would even like myself.

Being a young mother made me compassionate and loving and kept me striving towards success. My career faceplants over the years taught me perseverance and overcoming adversity. All of these things contributed to the woman I now am, and I wouldn't want to be any other way.

Love at First Sight

I am very transparent.

I often ask for forgiveness instead of permission and always say what's on my mind.

In fact, I have a tendency to say things before thinking them through.

The first time I met my husband wasn't any different. Our introduction was not smooth, and he still talks about it to this day.

I remember looking at this handsome creature as I was approaching him near the rec hall of the campground, and saying, "Who the hell are you?"

I guess that is what flies out of your mouth when you take a larger-than-life teenager and introduce her to the person she knows instantly is her soulmate.

Even though we met when I was fifteen, it wasn't until much later that we started dating. That didn't stop me from knowing he was the one for me. *He may be a little older than me now, but eventually, that wouldn't matter,* I thought in my head as I awaited his response.

He told me that his name was Bob. Instantly I regretted my choice of words, but it was too late to take them back.

It takes time to build trust, and some have an easier time with this than others. I use caution and let trust build. I had gotten pretty used to putting up a wall of defense, which is why I introduced myself that way to Bob. But I was truly interested in who he was despite how I talked to him.

When I saw Bob, I thought he was the most beautiful boy I had ever seen. The butterflies in my chest must have altered my ability to act like a normal human being. I went home that night thinking, *out of all the things to say, why did I need to say that or be so forceful?* Most people would have said, "Nice to meet you. I am so and so."

But I guess he must have liked it.

We have been married for over nineteen years now.

Not only did my forcefulness not scare him off, but my straightforward approach was the start of something amazing.

Our story begins at a campground where our families owned camping lots. My family and I would visit on the weekends, and that's how I ran into him. Neither of us was looking for love.

On the weekends, my family and I would escape the normal hustle of life with our version of camping, which was really "glamping" as we did not sweat it out in a tent. Instead, we had a modern camper equipped with a full-size bathroom and shower, kitchen, and air conditioning.

Back then, the campground was a place to hang out, and parents trusted their kids to roam free. We didn't have cell phones to distract us or occupy our entire day. Instead, we entertained ourselves.

We drove golf carts for transportation even though we were underage, swam until we were hungry, partied until the sun came up, and were no longer coherent, then slept a few hours and started it all over again.

I often remind myself of these times so that I can warn my kids about how quickly becoming an adult happens. The level of responsibility shifts so quickly after your teenage years are over, and suddenly the innocence and freedom of youth are gone.

I remember sneaking out to a party with my then friend, soon-to-be-boyfriend, and now my husband. It's a night

I will remember forever. This was the night that I knew he was the one.

We hadn't started dating at this point, but I had more than "just a friend" feelings for him. We had both been drinking a little too much and had to stop ourselves from laughing as we pushed his parents' golf cart backward out of his driveway so that we could go for a ride in the rain. We were soaked as the rain poured down on us, and all I could think about was how badly I wanted to kiss him, but I couldn't find the courage to do so.

His crystal blue eyes captured me in the rain that night. But I was too scared of losing my friend. I didn't have the courage to make a move with him. I carry the image of him that rainy night in my head to this day. It was the moment that changed everything for me.

I hadn't been exactly truthful with my parents about where I was that night. They were under the impression that I was staying at a friend's. I guess I didn't really stray too far from the truth since we did end up at a friend's camper. While tightly nestled on his chest and listening to his heartbeat as he fell asleep, I realized I wanted to be wrapped in his arms forever.

I still feel this way, so many years later, and I know just how lucky I am. I may have failed a million times over in virtually every other aspect of life, but my marriage isn't one of them.

I consider my first true success as allowing myself to trust this cute young boy. We would gather together as a large group of friends, but would always find each other in the party, and I think we both planned it that way. The fact is, I was just driven to him. His quiet nature intrigued me, and no matter where we ended up for the night or what crazy trouble we got into; I always looked for him if he wasn't already with me. He was the one person who would wait for me to roll out of bed.

I still remember my father yelling at me to wake up because that boy was coming around asking for me. As I grew older and began driving, our relationship was less of a weekend thing and more of an entire summer thing.

I can't remember defining our relationship; it just sort of happened and never ended. That's the thing about being best friends with the opposite sex; at some point, you become so in sync with one another that it is hard to not develop feelings beyond friendship. Bob and I already spent every day talking to each other; we just fell in love along the way. That love would grow stronger every year.

I do not believe that our lives crossed by accident.

I know in my heart that he was and is my soulmate; that we were meant to find each other. To him, I do not have imperfections. Those are my own insecurities. And I know we are stronger together because of our combined imperfections and how they relate to raising children and tackling life.

Who I am complements him in every way and vice-versa. I am extremely impatient, and he has all the patience in the world. I have a hard time containing my emotions, and he easily says only what he means. Together we balance each other out.

We grew up together.

Our dreams became something we envisioned as one throughout the years.

He has seen me at my worst, and he has seen me accomplish things I never thought were possible—all while standing by my side and supporting me endlessly.

I do not want to make it sound like it is easy because marriage is not easy. We are not the same people, but I am just as invested in him as he is in me. That is what makes us work.

A Surprise!

When Bob and I were dating, I was enrolled in the local community college to study nursing, ready to tackle the next phase of my life.

But here's the crazy part, I hate the sight of blood.

I am the mom who passes the peroxide to her husband because she can't bear the sharp cry of a baby in pain. I don't like open wounds or gashes, so this whole "I need to find a career with schooling" threw me into a direction that I was never going to excel at.

I was heading into a degree in nursing, and it was just not for me. I was leaping into courses for the sake of doing something because we were taught in school that the only real chance you had at surviving in this world was to go to college. I believed what I was told. And no, I am not against college by any means; I just don't think college is the right path for everyone. It wasn't the right path for me.

My life centered around working in retail during the day and going to community college at night. The schedule only lasted a few short months. I couldn't hack the long hours and found myself falling asleep at night. When I could no longer keep my eyes open, my professor would catch me dozing off and remind me that the class was only going to benefit me if I chose to participate.

I knew the hours were long, but I wasn't working at the retail place at the crack of dawn, and I was a 19-year-old kid. I had absolutely no reason to be falling asleep in class in the prime of my life.

That's when the lightbulb went off.

Could I be pregnant?

Without even mentioning it, Bob called me out. He knew before I took a test that I was carrying his baby.

Life changed quick.

I was now pregnant with my oldest son and could no longer keep up working and going to school.

So, I dropped out of college. The hardest part of being a college dropout was the disappointment and ridicule I got from others, including my own family. I was nineteen and living on my own, but somehow my family made sure I understood I'd just made the biggest mistake of my life.

It was never a mistake to me.

Even though my family thought my situation was shameful, they urged Bob and me to get married.

But I refused to set a wedding date while I was pregnant. My refusal came at a price. My family did not contribute to my wedding at all. My mom didn't even shop with me for my wedding dress, despite the fact that I was paying.

Their rejection left a deep scar, and the thing about scars is, they may heal, but they are always visible. Our skin thickens, and we press on, but they are still there.

The kicker is that the surprise people thought was unplanned was actually planned.

We were engaged and thought it might take some time to conceive. In actuality, it took me three days. So while the timing was earlier than expected, it wasn't anything that we hadn't planned for or that we couldn't handle.

We knew the risks when I went off my birth control. The result of that choice was one of the greatest gifts of my life. Nine months later, via cesarean section, we welcomed a gorgeous, healthy baby boy. After he had a bit of fetal distress, my baby emerged absolutely perfect.

By this time, my parents had come to terms with the fact that I was going to have a baby, and they were overjoyed with their first grandchild. But even that joyous event didn't change their mind about wanting to participate in the wedding.

A part of me didn't care.

It didn't matter to me what anyone else thought when it came to this child; it wasn't about them. It was about him, and he was ours. What truly mattered was seeing how excited Bob was holding his son, Maycen, for the first time. These are the moments in life you carry with you. You don't remember every hard day at home or work, but rather the sketches of memories past that are engraved within.

My little man stared right back at me with my own eyes. The truth is, I couldn't have been any more in love with my child. This unbelievable baby of mine with his big brown eyes and olive skin was amazing.

It was an adjustment having a new baby, but nothing that we couldn't handle. While my husband spent both his days and nights working, with barely any sleep in between, he gave me the freedom to stay home with my firstborn—a time I am forever grateful for. We all make sacrifices when we are in relationships. This was his sacrifice for his new little family.

Looking back, I am not sure that I would have survived working while having a new baby, especially one who cried nonstop. If you have never had a colicky baby, please consider yourself to be one lucky-ass parent. The relentless crying will drive an already exhausted new parent absolutely crazy. Instead of being upset that he couldn't sleep after two shifts, Bob would jump right in to help with Maycen so that I could get some rest. It really does take a team to raise children. Bob has endless patience and seeing him with our son was the most beautiful sight.

This is love.

This was us.

One Christmas, I couldn't get Maycen to settle down. Nothing I did soothed him. I tried car rides, the washing machine, using the vacuum, consoling him, diaper changes, and baths. All of these different methods everyone suggested proved to be nothing but failures to ease my baby's troubles.

I ended up in the car with my screaming baby and driving him to my husband's second job. We walked in the door where he was working, and with tears in my eyes, I begged him for help. I will never ever forget what happened next.

In one swift move, Bob picked the baby up out of his carrier, and Maycen stopped crying immediately. Bob leaned over to me and smiled; the baby nuzzled against his chest. I was reminded of how lucky I was to have him in my life. And I couldn't help but chuckle. Lucky? Perhaps, but I wasn't feeling lucky at that moment. I was relieved. I had spent the entire day trying to soothe my son, and all Bob had to do was pick him up? *Are you kidding me?* Perhaps the calming nature of my husband was exactly what Maycen needed. After that encounter, I knew parenting was going to be a wild, unpredictable ride that the two of us would figure out together.

As our son continued to grow, so did our expenses.

I had been working for a little while when I was pregnant, but then had lost my job. I was also doing a really crappy job of playing house. Maycen and I would sing songs all day and play. *Forget the housework; where was the fun in that?*

The only thing that I was quite good at was being a mom. Being a mom requires you to be selfless, to put the needs of someone else ahead of your own. I was excellent at making others a priority.

I was a happy new mom, but I didn't yet have a clue where life was going to take me. Instead, I focused on just living in the moment, wondering what was next for me.

I refer to this time of my life as "lost with purpose." I had no idea where I was going, but I did have a little boy I adored. He gave me a purpose, and knowing that, I was confident I would find my way!

Another challenge that we faced as young parents was that we had just the one car between us. Raising a new baby with one vehicle, especially with Bob working two jobs, wasn't easy. I needed to figure that out. But I had no idea where to even start. Since I had never bought a car myself, it was intimidating.

The only experience I'd had with cars happened on my 16th birthday when my dad showed up outside my school with my dream car. Standing alongside a 1994 grayish purple Camaro was my father, waiting for me to find him. Although the parking lot was packed full of teenagers racing to flee school, he wasn't very hard to spot. I was getting a ride home from a friend and saw him in the parking lot as we were pulling out. I tell you what, if that had been me now, I would have pissed my pants, but at sixteen, I didn't have baby bladder!

I share this with you because the Camaro has always been my car. I knew at age ten that I would drive a

Camaro. I wanted it. So, like any good father who could help his kid in such a way would, he forced me to put aside money from my jobs early on so that I could have my dream car when I turned sixteen. He taught me to work my ass off shamelessly in pursuit of anything I dared to dream about having. This came in handy later in life.

But his favor, on the one hand, was a bit controlling. It was my car, but it was also leverage for him in the event I didn't follow the rules. I knew this game. He has always played it. It wasn't really my car.

My investment was real, but the moment I screwed up, it belonged to him. His name was on the note of a loan that I had paid but I would never ever get credit for it.

That warped experience was of no help to me when I needed wheels so desperately.

I was stuck with a new baby and no car. If I'd known back then what I know now, I would have done things differently. But teachers didn't teach anything about credit in school. How to get it, how to maintain it, how important it is.

For example, I didn't know that medical bills could be reported to credit. As far as the car went, I had assumed that I was getting credit for the payments that I had been making on my car for the two years I owned it. That was not the case at all.

I was scrambling to find a way to get a new car and fast, but there were obstacles at every turn. I bet you can guess what the car dealer told us when we went to buy another car. Yup. We needed a co-signer.

I begged my parents to help us finance a vehicle. My mom agreed, but I felt like there were always strings attached to any help I asked for, and this time wasn't any different. In exchange for them helping us secure the loan, my mom required that I clean her home once a week.

I felt trapped—like I was being used to get something out of me that I wouldn't willingly give otherwise. I have zero tolerance for possession by anyone, let alone being manipulated into doing something because of my responsibility to my son.

All I was trying to do was grow up and be responsible, but the fact was, I needed help.

I swore from that moment on that I wouldn't add any stipulations to the help I gave other people. I did not want to ever be that person. I am not sure what the lesson was my mom was trying to teach me, but that whole situation taught me that I had absolutely no idea how credit worked or where to even begin to rebuild it.

I had a few medical collections on my credit report and nothing else. I couldn't get credit cards or a loan, and I had no clue how to fix this thing!

Credit was never once a topic of conversation at home. So, if we are not given the proper tools at school or at home, how does one prepare for this moment?

That lesson would change my life.

It woke up the urge in me to help others who were in the same situation I was. If I was struggling with figuring all of this out, then I was sure other people had to be as well.

I may not have figured out how to get my car at that exact time, but I'd just found my calling in life.

CHAPTER 3

GETTING STARTED

"Behind every successful woman is herself."
~Unknown

I snatched up the phone book and circled every mortgage company near me because back then, we didn't have online search engines. And I needed a job and a car.

Our first baby was still a baby, but that didn't matter because we weren't making enough money, and my new priority had to be working.

Madden hadn't entered the picture yet, and unlike Maycen, he would make us wait to grace us with his presence.

I was determined to learn about credit because I had completely wrecked mine by not knowing how to maintain it. What better way to do that than to put myself smack in the middle of home loans? Because how could I get credit if no one would give me any credit?

I must have called a hundred mortgage companies before someone agreed to let me come in to interview. All I needed was a company that would hire me. I started preparing because I wasn't going to stop interviewing until I had a job. I had no idea how I was going to pull off landing a position with a company working in an industry I knew nothing about, but again, I was determined to make it happen.

I don't really remember what I said to get my foot in the door of that first mortgage company, but it must have been decent because I got the job!

It definitely helped that it was 2002, and the mortgage industry was HOT. It didn't take much to get a home loan in those days. If you had a job, credit wasn't really a qualifying factor. The standards today are most certainly not the standards when I was starting out.

The economy was booming, house prices were soaring, and I wanted in on that! Everyone was buying homes because they didn't need much credit. In fact, during that time, it was easier to buy a home than a car. Learning that fact was a true eye-opener for me. I was in shock at what I was seeing.

While some customers couldn't pay a car loan on time, we were giving them hundreds of thousands of dollars to buy a house. I might have been new to the industry and trying to absorb as much information as I could, but I also wasn't naive.

The company I was hired to work for was not really existent. My boss rarely showed up to the office, so it was the team members who trained me. I was learning how to take my outgoing personality and capture future clients with it.

When payday finally rolled around, it didn't take me long to figure out why the company owner rarely showed up to the office. Payday felt like a shakedown with our boss nowhere to be found. Our payday went from being on a regular schedule to only being paid when he got paid. To make matters worse, if we held our checks for longer than a day and didn't take them directly to the bank they were drawn from, they would bounce. Looking back on it now, I can see that job as a learning experience, but at the time, it was hard to appreciate that.

No matter how many loans we closed, it was the same story. "Good luck cashing your check," all the other employees and I would tell each other on payday. We all knew we had to be at the owner's bank before anyone else if we wanted to collect what was due, so that is exactly what we did.

As soon as he'd sign the checks, we'd go straight to his bank to get our money in hand. It was the only way we could be sure to get paid. Clearly, this wasn't an ideal situation, but those who worked with me really did like their jobs. We just had to make a business move for the sake of our sanity and pocketbooks.

Racing each other to the bank didn't create a calm working environment, but we were sticking with each other, and that was crucial because of what happened next.

Eventually, all three employees (including myself) set out to find a mortgage company that would let us open up our own branch. Keep in mind that I was a few months into learning the entire mortgage game, yet I was requesting a partnership to establish a branch with two co-workers. Talk about lady balls. I look back and laugh at how brazen I was. But, in my life so far, all I have known is that effort outweighs talent when talent doesn't perform.

In a matter of six months, I'd talked my way into a job that I wasn't well qualified for. Despite that, I had managed to earn the respect of my co-workers while negotiating a sister mortgage branch of our own to run.

At this point, all the training that I'd had only covered the basics: how to prepare an application for clients, how to meet with them, and how to close a loan. That was it.

Luckily I was born with an insane desire to succeed, and I researched everything to try to teach myself what it was that I needed to know. My partners and lenders were great support along the way. I paid attention to what the requirements were on every approval I received for a client, and repetition was key. That meant the more loans I got, the easier it got.

When my partners and I were on the hunt for an office location, I knew just the place—although we were still in awe that what we had put in motion was actually working.

Ironically enough, my father owned a commercial building where he ran his company, and it was right in the area where we were looking. The building had endless possibilities for office space, so once again, I found myself going to my father for help. Typically, in a commercial property rental, you are responsible for the build-out, but I brought the missing piece to the team.

The rest of my team and I didn't have the funds to build out a rental to meet our needs as a company. We needed offices and separation so that our clients would feel safe during an extremely personal exchange of information.

I had a connection to solving our location challenge, but I also had a lack of funds. Luckily for our little team, my father built out a space for our new business endeavor.

Some kids ask their parents to pay for college, not me.

I asked mine to help fund a build-out on a location for a new business, and my dad did it. He is a dreamer too. I knew I was better off getting his help this way. Asking Dad for money wasn't going to get me anywhere with him. But asking him to help me build a career was a completely different story. I marched myself into his office to pitch him the idea knowing that he would bite.

Once the new office was up and running, I would spend my days chatting it up with clients, account executives, and lenders. One account executive, in particular, used to visit the office often and intrigued me with his sales role.

I loved mortgages, but I wanted to learn how an underwriter thought and what they wanted, so I could be proactive and not reactive. Not knowing what was going to be asked of a client made me feel like I was doing the work backward. I wanted all the information on what we were asking for before I took the request to the person trying to secure the loan.

Each time he would come to visit, I would be so envious, and while I loved the loan officer side of the business, I couldn't predict what I needed for clients and so felt that I was not very good at my job.

I started to question if I was in the right position. Not because of the industry or the mortgage field so much, because I did love it, but because I felt like I needed to better understand my position.

I didn't make any sudden movements, but I wasn't closing enough loans to justify having the overhead of a business. I felt the burden of that every day and hadn't been introduced to Marketing 101 (and this was long before the days of social media). Eventually, the tension of being unable to close enough was felt in the office, and it would separate the team that taught me so much.

Then one day I called up the account executive I admired the most and asked him for a job. I could see the writing on the wall. It was a great run, but I had a desperate need to explore the roles available in the mortgage industry.

Since I wanted to know what an underwriter thought and lacked that puzzle piece, I figured, *what better way to learn that than to work directly with them.* I knew if I moved to a wholesale position, that was exactly what I would be doing.

It took me a few solid months of asking about underwriting opportunities before the account executive connected me with the owner of his company for an interview.

I still remember requesting that interview like it was yesterday, knowing that it was an amazing opportunity to grow, and being so nervous that I was shaking.

Maybe it was nerves or perhaps excitement; either way, I wasn't giving in until I secured an opportunity to discuss a position and get exactly what I wanted.

After all, opportunity doesn't just come to you; you have to go out and create it yourself. I needed to seize the moment.

By then, I had two years of working in mortgages under my belt, so I knew the industry, but my experience was in origination, not processing—the job I was seeking.

This company had no reason to hire me for a position in processing, but I went to the interview anyway, knowing full well I had to do whatever was necessary to secure the job. Besides that, I wanted it.

When I want something, I go all in. This job was no exception. With my persistence, I knew I could surely land it.

My goal was to learn as much as I could and put a ton of pressure on myself to nail the next chapter in my life.

As a small-town country girl with a big personality, I was ready to take on the world. Walking into the office for my interview, I felt sick. After all, I was determined, but not fearless…yet.

I remember an office filled with files and a smooth-talking Italian man who introduced himself as the owner of the company. He complimented me on my accomplishments despite my short time in the business and seemed almost in awe at how I'd landed a branch at such a young age. I think I reminded him of himself.

He was a master of words and quickly captivated my attention by pointing out that I was well-suited for the processing job. I also think that he saw me as a bit of a project. I had a lot to learn, but my desire landed me the interview, and I couldn't help but believe that my persistence would land me the job.

During the interview, we discussed my experience and intentions of making this new potential career my life path. His face was easily readable, proving that I was saying what he wanted to hear. I showed my commitment to the position by addressing his reservation about the commute.

It was over an hour and a half each way, so I understood his concern. But I was prepared for that; I was going to do whatever I needed to do so that I could learn the processing side of the mortgage industry.

I spoke of my small town and the limited availability of jobs in that area. Yes, the town had grown a lot over the years, but there wasn't a market for lenders. If I wanted to play in the mortgage game, the only option was to travel. When I told him that it was enough to win him over and secure the job.

Once I had nailed the interview, I had to report back to my parents that what they had built for me was going to be closed down, and as you can imagine, that didn't go over very well. I am sure they were quite disappointed but excited for me at the same time. They realized that what I was embarking on was a big opportunity and chose to focus on that.

By this time, the team had been driven apart, and we were all heading in different directions. I was the only one who remained. But I didn't feel abandoned; I felt that it was time to move on and let it be what it was—a great learning experience.

I remember thinking I had hit the jackpot because I could boast a salary for the first time in my twenty-two years. I had never earned anything more than a meagerly hourly wage. My husband and I celebrated the new opportunity! It was the third big milestone in our lives together. The first being our baby and then our marriage. Now I had landed a new job that came with a decent living.

The career milestone was for me, but the life-changing results benefitted our young family. With this new job, I felt as if I could finally dive in and learn why certain things were required to secure a loan. I could explain to other brokers what was necessary to get their clients approved.

My fellow processors who were beside me every day were much more experienced than I was, and I had a lot of catching up to do, so I put my head down and listened. I soaked it all in like a sponge as I listened to every conversation they had. They would teach me the value of a business relationship and how to maintain it. And they proved to be not just excellent cube mates and trainers, but they hit the phones hard and worked as fast as they could to review thousands of documents a day to meet closing date deadlines.

The questions and challenges flew at them, and I had a close-up view of how they solved them, which in turn provided the means for me to be able to combat the same. I think I expected my new career to be in a field I could master quickly, but that couldn't be any farther from the truth.

Yes, I loved every second of what I did, and my experience proved to be where I got my first real start in the industry. I was also grateful that I'd closed the location back home. I worked hard to make sure that I earned my keep.

Besides seeking the perfect job, Bob and I had also been trying—unsuccessfully—for another child for three long years. Looking back, it probably just wasn't in the cards at the moment. It was my time to focus on my career and see where my new job would take me. But I remember being absolutely devastated every single month that I wasn't pregnant. My dream was that my boys would play on the same baseball team. But as the years slipped by, so did that dream.

My new job became a distraction from the heartache of wanting another baby. I eventually stopped crying every month and came to terms with the fact that I was only meant to have one child. It is not an easy thing to do—especially when you are young and already have a kid.

Also, not easy is enduring the habit that people have of making small talk when they see you. "When are you guys going to have another one?" was all Bob and I would hear. No one was intentionally trying to make me sad by asking that, but when you are trying to have a baby, and you hear that question, it's hard. I wished for nothing more than a society that thought before they said anything that could hurt a family actively trying for a baby without success.

I felt as if all of life's pieces were starting to fall into place, with the exception of having a baby. So, I finally decided to stop letting myself get worked up over not getting pregnant, and I trusted that having a baby would fall into place, too.

My husband had sacrificed his career for mine. He allowed me the freedom to explore what I wanted to do while he stayed close to home for Maycen. Anything he did for a job had to have flexible hours. This was him giving in. This man, the one my parents argued with me endlessly about, always chose my needs over his. Two of us couldn't travel; one of us needed to remain close to home for the sake of our little guy, so he volunteered to be that parent. I often wonder if I stole from him what he needed in his professional life.

I think Bob noticed the passion that I had, and he wanted to give me the chance to live my dream. I needed to go down my career path to satisfy my craving to reach my personal goals, development, and growth. That meant any ambitions he had were put on hold while I spread my wings.

Compromising for the sake of each other is the basis of any solid marriage.

My husband has sacrificed way more than I ever give him credit for. His time, his career dreams, and life goals were delayed for me. Not because he owed it to me, but because he supported me.

That is love. That is the man that I married. And all of those imperfections that I see in myself, he doesn't. In his eyes, nothing can stand in the way of me accomplishing what I set out to do. Knowing he feels that way gives me more self-confidence and has allowed me to soar to levels in life that set my soul on fire!

My son, who was so young at the time, didn't seem to be phased by seeing me less than he was used to. My new job required a three-hour-a-day commute—three hours a day that I gave up being with him. He was so in love with his daycare provider that he was extremely happy during the time I was gone, despite the fact that I left for work every morning feeling guilty, thinking my schedule might have a negative effect on him somehow. It didn't, and now that he is grown, he refers to that time as some of the best years of his life.

I beat myself up every day for leaving him, but it was completely unnecessary because he was just fine. He was off singing his ABC's and collecting gold stars for good behavior—exactly what he needed to do to grow. He needed that as much as I needed a sense of accomplishment in the workplace. Still, at the time, I thought I was the worst mother in the world.

How I felt was extremely common.

As mothers, we often beat ourselves up for no good reason and terrify ourselves with unnecessary worry. It's the one thing that I wish I could change about myself. We develop what I call "mom guilt" from spending time away from our kids and family, and no matter how much we try, we cannot suppress that feeling. As women with children, progressing in our careers and in life, the daily responsibility does not diminish, but the time in which we are able to tackle every responsibility sure does.

At the time, I worked more than ever and only had the weekends to be with my family, and the struggle of that seemed unbearable. The weekday evenings of bath time and dinner making were replaced with traffic and congested highways.

A mother feels the pressure of everything in life.

If I am selfishly working on pursuing my life goals, I tend to feel the need to accommodate my kids in some sort of way.

It was the same when I was working those long hours, and there was only Maycen at home. Instead of teaching him new things, I wanted to spoil him at the store or take him to the movies.

But that mentality had to change. We don't owe our kids because we want to have a career and having a career doesn't make us selfish. It makes us expert multi-taskers.

I am telling you this because my kids are older, and I promise you, they are okay. If you are working a lot, your kids won't grow up resenting you at all. They will grow up inspired to chase their life goals.

I want you to hear me when I tell you that kids grow up just fine no matter where you work and no matter how many hours you work. You are raising champions who see the true grit of your sacrifices. Learn to embrace that because you don't really see how much it helps them grow until they are almost adults—their childhoods long passed.

If you are not careful about shaming yourself, you could spend the best years of their lives trying to overcompensate for something that only exists in your mind.

CHAPTER 4

FINDING MY STRENGTH

"She is both hellfire and holy water, and the flavor you taste depends on how you treat her." ~Sneha Pal

I was someone's wife and a mother to one very happy and loving little boy who was older now. I had found clarity in my everyday purpose. I wasn't that teenage girl who was carefree and overconfident any longer. It is crazy how your child's little hand that fits so perfectly in your palm is such a big driving force in your motivation.

Life was no longer just about me. It was time to discover all that I was capable of for the sake of the child that I'd brought into this world. I was committed to bettering myself on his behalf. My focus couldn't have been any clearer, and that made me cautious and protective. I might have still been young by society's standards as I was in my early twenties, but I was no longer a self-possessed, reckless young lady.

Well, maybe I was a little reckless and carefree, but not nearly as much as I had been. Motherhood doesn't define us, but it sure as hell makes us grow up.

Instead of worrying about what party I was heading off to, I was worried about how I was going to plan for Maycen's college one day and what steps I was going to take to help him accomplish his goals. My boys changed my life. I simply wouldn't be where I am today without them.

Unfortunately, adulting comes with its share of compromise. My tradeoff for wanting to achieve my goals was working an hour and a half away from home in my processor job.

Some days I cursed the fact that the town I lived in didn't have jobs in my field. I missed baseball practices and so many snuggles with my young son. Missing him constantly for the sake of providing a good life for him felt a lot like making a deal with the devil. After all, it was time I would never get back.

My snuggles were replaced by his daddy's arms being wrapped around him and one very early alarm sounding in the background in the morning for me.

With great sacrifice comes great reward. Following my ambition, I noticed small changes and an ease in daily living expenses. It was the beginning of living comfortably, and the feeling of security is priceless. I could see a future for him finally. It became easier to say goodbye in the morning as he adjusted to his daycare quicker than I adjusted to leaving him. Coming to terms with missing your child isn't always easy, and that is okay.

My advice to you is to take this one step at a time. Quit punishing yourself because you do not stay at home; sometimes, women NEED to work, and that is something you should not feel guilty about.

In my new career, it was time to show the world that I was capable. If I was going to miss time with my son, it had better be worth it, and I believed that it was.

The climb is never easy, but you will never regret it.

During the rise, it felt as though I was never going to learn all the different aspects of the job. This wasn't college, and I wasn't in a room full of professors who were teaching me step by step. I didn't earn a four-year degree, so I had to learn on the fly and not only acquire the necessary knowledge and skills needed, but I also had to excel in this new environment that was completely foreign to me.

There I was in a packed room full of others who shared the same job title, and had the same conversations, and they moved fast. Everything went so fast at times I couldn't keep up. But I had to work faster and make fewer mistakes if this was going to work.

This was a fast-paced industry that demanded perfection each and every day. As much as I learned, it was still hard to be learning and perfect at the same time. I had gathered bits and pieces of what I was expected to do, but when you only know half of what that really entails, you tend to draw the unwanted attention of every manager and can accumulate some pretty awkward glares in your direction. Even then, I didn't believe in excuses and took my ass-chewings for my missteps along the way.

This is where humility comes into play. I could have walked away, insisting my managers were mean to me, but where is the growth in that? The only way we learn is by making mistakes and holding ourselves accountable for those mistakes.

It was truly embarrassing to have my work examined by someone else and find that I hadn't quite nailed it, but I refused to give in and back down. I found myself apologizing profusely with the promise that time would make me better.

One thing that I can say during this growth period is that my cubemates tried to help as much as they could. They saw me grinding every single day and believe me when I tell you that the quality of persistence is appreciated by all who work with you.

If people see that you are giving it your everything, they are more tolerant and will try to help you. If you simply do not give a shit, you don't stand a chance. I was a project, and they never gave up on me because I didn't give up on myself.

At work, I sat me next to a father of three and a tough gal from New York. These two would spend their days providing support for me while doing their own jobs. If they were frustrated, they didn't show it. And they kept my spirits up even after it was clear that I was in over my head. The worst part of this time was that I didn't get training. This was survival mode: sink or swim. I was quick to jump back on my feet and refused to see anything but what would be my eventual triumph.

I tell you all of this humbly because none of us are perfect and sometimes the hardest moments in life are the ones that force us to find our strength. In doing so, these moments shape us for who we will later become.

I may not have been amazing at my new job, but it didn't take long for me to feel like I fit in. I'm pretty sure my manager never really adored me, but I wasn't at the same level as her seasoned team members, and she had every right to be annoyed. After all, she hadn't hired me; the owner had.

I never had any dealings with the owner again after he hired me, but it seemed as though he genuinely cared for all of us, which I truly admired. Employees who are appreciated make your customer feel appreciated, and that, in turn, will construct greatness.

Despite being on the radar for all my mistakes, I brought my ass into work every single day, even though it was an hour and a half each way. At lunchtime, I ate a can of soup at my desk because *who had time to eat lunch?*

Tenacity and falling forward were my mantra. I didn't back down from a challenge or allow fear to drive my decisions. I was relentless and gained my strength along the way because of it. This was a whole new feeling for me. I might be failing, but I was definitely making forward progress.

I had gotten used to criticism as a teenager for being stubborn when my parents or teachers couldn't control me. Up until this point, I had spent so much of my life apologizing for being relentless, for being loud, and forceful, and stubborn—the very same qualities I needed at that exact moment in my life, I had been told to suppress.

I am so glad that I never compromised who I was because those skills allowed me to step up my game. I continued to push through with my head held high until the nasty stares turned into pats on the back. It was an amazing feeling given how far I had come over a span of six months.

Even though I was gradually improving, no matter how great I was becoming, I still fell short of the team's talent level. I was still being coached by management because once you are on that "no-no watch list," it is very hard to take yourself off. But that didn't stop me; I was going to learn the job come hell or high water.

Pride aside, I chose to develop a relationship with my sales team, who I was directly responsible for each day. It was my job to close their loans and make them money. I was paired up with an account executive who, ironically, lived in the same small town as me. This proved to be a blessing in disguise because my car was about to see its final days.

I had saved some money, but not enough, and I had yet to learn the skills necessary to improve my credit score. It took years to repair the damage that I had done.

But I was soon without a car and needed to act fast. That was hard to do when every place that would sell me a decent car required a substantial down payment to grant me credit. Even with that substantial down payment, I was in a helpless position. The lower the credit score, the more interest they would charge.

My friend and co-worker drove me back and forth to work every single day until I found a new ride, and I never missed one shift, even with a broken car.

Knowing this situation couldn't last forever, I simply didn't have a choice but to put every penny toward the purchase of a really old vehicle that I couldn't stand and that had an insane payment due to the interest.

I desperately needed a win and hoped that one would come my way.

My new job came with a huge learning curve, but I was determined not to let the negativity at work with management change my overall goals. We all cross paths with people who can't stand us, and that is okay. Never once did I take any of my manager's harsh words or dirty looks personally. I was underperforming, and she had every right to her feelings and reactions, although it was painful.

The other seasoned processors ran circles around me. Everyone had vast knowledge of the business, and I had very little. Of course, it was easier for them. I took every second to research where I was making my mistakes so that I could learn from them.

In all my years in this business, I've learned that very few people are willing to assume responsibility, and even fewer take the time to develop their skills before throwing in the towel. Of course, it is going to be hard, and it will force you to face your shortcomings, but the end result and overcoming your struggles is worth the pain.

Excuses allow you to place blame; accountability allows for personal development.

If you do not know what you are doing wrong because you never assume you are at fault, you will continuously make the same mistakes. You can't be successful if you are unwilling to take action, and that always means evaluating yourself and making adjustments along the way.

We are human, and because of that, we are extremely critical of ourselves. I am no different. I promise you that the haters have nicer things to say about me than I do about myself. I am never satisfied when it comes to self-improvement. It doesn't matter how many loans I close; I will always want to close one more and implement new strategies to allow for that—that's because the feeling of helping someone purchase a new home is unlike any other feeling I have ever experienced. It is demanding, inspiring, frustrating, intense, and gratifying.

You can't be upset with the results you didn't get due to the effort you didn't put into your job. You need to work for it. Nothing great in life comes without effort. Even the opportunities we seek are a direct result of our actions.

I knew I had put myself out there and had taken a risk for the sake of bettering myself. I was going to eventually crush my performance.

My time with this company was a short-lived experience. At just around a year, right when I was really starting to get my feet wet, I was let go. They were done helping me grow. I was asked to seek excellence elsewhere.

I wasn't even upset, but I was thankful for the opportunity even though it didn't end well for me.

Truth be told, they probably tried to make it as miserable as possible, but I wouldn't give them the satisfaction of quitting. I know my direct manager was not a huge fan of mine, and I was beginning to understand that I did not fit in so well with her team. The rest of the employees had way more experience, and the uptrain is not easy in this field. So I do not blame them for this move because it led to my next move.

At the time, companies in the mortgage field were hiring like crazy and throwing myself into a career there would prove to be the best thing I could do for myself.

This time when I was searching for a new job, I had more experience and knew exactly what I was going to do. I was going to keep fighting because I really enjoyed the chaos of the industry.

Remember that fearless risk-taker? She was still in there, and a challenge was exactly what she liked.

This was a career that I could see myself working in forever, and it was fulfilling. To be a part of something so important to a family's future never gets old.

The only thing that I didn't like about the processing side of the industry was being removed from the direct client relationship. In processing, I was just someone on the other end of the phone dealing with someone else who was speaking for the buyer. I had to remind myself that I was doing this for the sake of providing a stable income for my family and to improve at the job that I'd once had. One day I would return to originating mortgages, and when I did, I would be so much better for it.

But at this point, I was stuck contemplating my next move. I knew that I wanted to keep being an account manager/loan processor. Until I mastered it, I wasn't going back to my previous job of being a loan officer, and I hadn't mastered the "why" that surrounded the underwriter's decision.

I wanted to be able to think like an underwriter so that I could prepare my clients before their loans were underwritten on the front end. As I mentioned, the jobs were plentiful, and the economy was booming. It didn't take me long to seek my excellence somewhere else.

The very next day, after being let go from the company, I was set to interview with another mortgage company. But I had to move fast; there was no time to waste. Even though I had only been with my prior company a year, I had developed relationships with many of the people I worked with, and my connections had served me well. One call to a former employee landed me an interview on the spot with another mortgage company.

Here is how crazy life can work out sometimes.

The morning I was fired, my nerves were a little worked, I had no idea how I was going to explain what had happened to my husband. Then I started to feel ill. We all get that sick feeling in the pit of our stomachs that won't subside when we are panicked. I brushed it off, knowing that it had been a long day. But come nighttime, I was throwing up like crazy! I couldn't hold anything down. I didn't want to think about food, see it or smell it. This was not fear of the unknown, making me vomit. This was not an unsettling feeling of plotting my next move. If you are a mom, you know exactly where this is going.

I ran off to the local pharmacy to buy a test, and sure enough, I was pregnant! The whole time we had been trying for a baby, I had been gainfully employed. Now I was fired and pregnant all in one day. There was no time to sit around and cry about losing my job; I had a job interview to nail!

My life had just gotten even more real since we now had one more mouth to feed. One more person was counting on me to make something of myself. This baby I now carried was a symbol of everything good in my life. It was a sign of encouragement to keep pushing forward despite the setback of losing my job. This baby was the best blessing.

I had spent the first year of "trying" absolutely crushed and crying in disappointment after I would get my period. After one more year of hoping but not emotionally investing myself in the possibility of having another baby, I was now three solid years into trying to have a baby.

I had changed my mindset from being sad about it and had worked on myself and my career to provide a better life for my family. Life has a funny way of working out like that. I did not focus on having a baby, but one day it just happened. There was only one snag; I needed to land a job and fast! I needed health insurance.

That week, I lined up a few other interviews with other companies. But I wanted the reassurance to know that I was making the right decision. We were not going to be a family of three any longer; there would be four of us. It was about to get expensive. Guess what else came with the news of us expecting another baby finally? Another reason to slay my goals. The motivation continued to grow as my family did.

During one interview, I was greeted by a less-than-enthused callus woman who quite frankly terrified me. I could tell that she had formed an opinion of me within minutes of our meeting, and I hadn't given her the impression I had hoped for.

She proceeded to tell me that she wanted the VP to do an interview with me as well after disapprovingly looking over my resume and pounding me with questions. I followed her to an adjacent room to attempt to save what I had just clearly wrecked.

I knew in that moment that I had better put my big girl pants on and figure this out. She ran off without telling me where she was going, but she didn't go far. I spent another twenty minutes going over my career story in a different way. I had to impress this man who was to walk in the door any minute.

But I was so nervous; I was shaking. When the VP walked in, he smiled and thanked me before telling me that he was going to speak with the lady who had initially interviewed me. After he left and had stepped into the office next door, I heard her voice coming through the open door, discussing how she wasn't sure if she wanted to hire me. She didn't like me.

The back and forth went on for a little bit, and I heard every single word they said about me—none of them nice. Here is the thing about me; I will do whatever I can do to prove that your theory of who I am isn't even close to the actual me.

This woman clearly thought I had no business being there. So, when the time came for the VP to come back after speaking with her, I held nothing back. I had one chance.

Instead of trying to prove that I was capable and ignoring the unfortunate conversation I'd just heard, I chose to bring it out into the open.

I led with, "It is a pleasure to meet you, and I couldn't help but overhear your conversation because I am sitting outside your open-door meeting. It seems that her interest in me is less than favorable, but I can assure you that I am quite capable of adapting to a different role and rising under pressure." That talk sealed the deal, and after my interview, I was hired.

Not only did the VP hire me, but he paired me with the lady who didn't want me. Isn't that life? I had just been fired by a company only to be placed on a team where the manager clearly hated me. I could already tell she wasn't going to take it easy on me. But I thought *that's okay. All it does is make me tougher.*

The new job was amazing, and I felt larger than life. I had received a $10,000 a year raise and was expecting another baby. When the job offer was extended to me, I graciously accepted and slept like a baby that night!

That job was easily one of the favorites of my career. It was not clear of challenges by any means, but I was a 23-year-old kid with a career in mortgages at a time when the industry was booming! This job came with additional responsibilities because the office did things a little differently.

My position was a processing/underwriting role. Meaning, from the time a file was received, I was responsible for all of it. I was the eyes of the deal, and if I didn't do my job, the loan file wouldn't close on time, and the families I was helping would suffer.

The company had hired a quality control department to review our files for completeness prior to closing. Just before closing means you better have everything in order, or you are not closing, and then you are calling a bunch of angry people to postpone and ask for more documentation.

Not only was I starting with a new company, but I was doing the job of what had been divided between two people at my last company.

At my previous position, I would hand the file off, and someone else would be responsible for making sure all of the items needed for the loan sale were secured. Now, I had to do that, as well. I do love a good challenge, so I was right back to where I was before— learning on the fly how to be the best I could be, under a manager who wasn't fond of me.

I was again outside my comfort zone. Here is what I will tell you about a comfort zone. Nothing good comes from it. I may have needed some serious coaching, but the experience that I gained was irreplaceable. Sure, I was told that I wasn't good enough, time and time again. Sure I received almost the same dirty looks from my new manager that my old manager had given me when I made eye contact with her. You know, the accusing ones that say, "If I could fire you today, I would. I hope you get tired of my dirty looks and snotty remarks and just quit." But I showed up, again and again, every single day, to prove her wrong.

I would develop some incredible relationships in the months to come, and it only secured my position there. My brokers, sales team, and I began crushing business. But, more loans equaled more mistakes that my quality control department caught. Still absorbing the order of what they needed, I had to learn to keep up and keep out in front of the damn red pen notes outlining my errors! The more red pen marks, the more my manager walked around with an attitude like *I told you that you shouldn't have hired her.*

It didn't take me long to find a way to overcome the challenges. It just required that I work at it, instead of letting the mistakes and my manager's attitude keep me from succeeding.

Shortly after I started at that job, we had a shift in management, and I was introduced to a manager I loved. She was helpful. She wanted me to succeed. Finally. It took a few managers who didn't like me and didn't want to help me succeed to get to this point, but I had a manager at last who really cared, and I worked equally hard for her.

Not long after that, my precious baby was born, and life got a bit crazy! Now Twenty-four with two kids, I had fast-forwarded my life into motherhood and being a provider. I spent way more time away from my family than I should have. The travel was insane, and I had to leave my baby five days a week for fourteen hours at a time each day. I consider myself very fortunate because my hubby stayed at home with our new baby boy. I didn't want my newborn in daycare, and I couldn't leave my job.

I was paid cash, monthly bonuses, and salary. Hell, my insurance was so good I paid for nothing after my son was born. I'm sure my husband felt very alone during my time with that company. It was a very difficult transition for us. He was less than thrilled about giving up his job so that I could pursue mine. He had already put so much of his life on hold so that I could achieve what I wanted in life, and here he was again making another sacrifice for me because I believed that our new son needed someone to bond with him. If I couldn't be home, I wanted Bob to be.

This arrangement caused quite a few fights over the years. The fact is that we just do the best that we can. Marriage is not all roses and sunshine. It is quite difficult at times because we have very different needs. Compromising can be difficult, and this was a big one for my husband.

With my demanding job and my long commute, I was tortured by all that I was missing in my kids' lives. All of the baseball games for my oldest, and giggles and snuggles with both sons. My husband really stepped up to the plate. He became the baseball coach to Maycen's team, except he didn't have the support of a wife who worked close to home, who could easily watch a young baby. In fact, he didn't have me at all, and neither did my kids.

So, he found himself coaching my oldest son and a team while managing a baby in a stroller. He was all by himself, and that led to more guilt for me.

Divide and conquer was what this stage of our lives was all about. It was nonstop work for me, and no home life, and it was juggling all things on the home front alone for my husband. At this point in my life, I felt as if I were an outsider looking in on my family. I was disconnected from them. Despite my desire to step in when I was home, those moments were so few and far between that I felt as if I were out of place in my own home—as if I didn't even know my kids or my own husband. I was home enough to go to sleep, and that was about all. When I was there, it just felt as if I was in the way.

I remember lying awake at night, wondering if I was making the right decision and having a distinct inner battle over if I was providing for my family or if I was tearing them apart.

This went on for four years. I was hardly ever home. I rode a wave of insane production because anyone could get a loan back then, and it only intensified as the years went on. The work hours stretched later and later and later.

I am not one of those people who can quit for the night if I still have work to do, no matter how late it happens to be. I was making overtime money and lots of it. So, what do you do when you are making good money and have young kids?

I justified my guilty feelings by reminding myself that I had a responsibility to my family and my husband, who had already given up so much for me. I couldn't look him in the eye if I didn't make something of myself.

It wasn't all bad, because after all, with hard work comes great reward.

At the age of twenty-four, I had my youngest son and, soon thereafter, was able to purchase my first home. It was a little Cape Cod with a high interest rate on a combo loan. Meaning we had 100% financing on this home and no official skin in the game with any form of down payment. The loan was broken up into a first and second mortgage, which was quite common during that time.

Life was going as planned. Not only was I young and making good money, but I had fixed my broken credit; we'd had another baby that we had been desperately trying for and had just bought our first home. I was no longer that young girl begging anyone for help to buy a new vehicle. I could do that on my own. I had taken control of my life and done what I needed to do to thrive.

PART 2:
AFTER THE CRASH

CHAPTER 5

LOSING EVERYTHING AND FAITH

"If you lose money, you lose much. If you lose friends, you lose more. If you lose faith, you lose all." ~Eleanor Roosevelt

I continued to close mortgages and commute for another full year before the hot market shifted.

The fact is you can only continue down the path of destruction for so long before the chaos comes to an end.

We were dealing with all the buyers who were credit challenged but getting loans, the lack of qualifying necessary to buy a home in normal circumstances, and loan fraud. Combine that with the potential pulling of the plug on purchasing these loans, and we were all heading for some very turbulent times—even though everyone in the industry knew it would eventually happen. Like a typical 20-something, I hadn't saved any of the money I had worked so hard to earn. So life was about to teach me about responsibility, and I was going to learn from it.

By now, I was more knowledgeable in my career as I had five and a half years under my belt; I had learned about the markets and had enough experience to be a better loan officer should the opportunity present itself again.

My job at that time job taught me so much, but I could see the writing on the wall. You can't give people homes who don't pay their bills without suffering the consequences. It was just a matter of time before the market couldn't sustain those types of loans, but until that day actually came, we were under strict orders to push out as many mortgages as we possibly could.

I sat in so many meetings where we were told, "The market is okay, and we are okay." Yet, it was complete bullshit, and we all knew it. We also heard, "No one is in jeopardy of losing their jobs." This was more bullshit management kept feeding us that no one believed. The only thing we were left with was uncertainty and fear. After all, it wasn't that we were just losing our jobs; we were facing a complete lockdown of the industry. All we could do was ride the wave until it was over.

I focused on working my ass off and cashing every check that I was paid. Our staff was heavy in a declining market, and we all became a salary drain on the business's pocketbook. It didn't take my company long to start diminishing their workforce, and I was caught up in that.

I understood where my career was headed at the time, but what I failed to realize was the effect being let go would have on my life. Yes, business would come to a staggering halt, but I never predicted the amount of financial devastation it would cause my family and the rest of the country. I suffered long before most others.

I had been employed in an industry that was about to cause some serious havoc. My job would be the first to be cut, and that started the relentless cycle of turmoil of epic proportions in the economy. When you are the leader, usually, there is a reward.

In this case, coming in first didn't pay off. To stop the bleeding of the value loss on homes, banks assisted borrowers by modifying their home loans to prevent the rapid spread of inducing further hardship. That option didn't exist for me at the time. We didn't have help. Not that I would have wanted any help anyway. The help that was eventually extended resulted in large, heavy payments in the form of a second mortgage, and in some cases, it was payable after the modification period. Who is saving to pay that lump sum back during a period of financial upheaval? I wasn't.

It was time to decide if I would continue to travel, stay in the industry, and fight for a job in a field that was under extreme scrutiny. My job required me to be away from my family. Was it time to throw in the towel, or should I opt to seek excellence somewhere else?

I chose the latter.

What was the alternative? Sit and cry about it? I didn't have time for that; I had to worry about my kids. But I knew one thing for sure; I was tired of traveling. I welcomed a break, and I really needed to be with my children. I had already missed out on so much of their lives—so many baseball and basketball games and school events. My lifestyle put a ton of pressure on my husband. It was almost as if he were a single parent. It was time for me to try something else and step up on the home front. After all, *we could figure it out, right?* It couldn't be all that bad.

But, I had no idea just how wrong I was about this next chapter in my life.

I sought out remote loan processor positions from brokers. I can't say this was a smart thing to do, but it was a job. Unfortunately for me, it was one that I didn't like so much. I worked for a group of lazy loan officers. Not that I minded cleaning up messes but making very little money doing it was frustrating. I was barely closing any loans because of all the changes that were going on with the banking industry, and there weren't close to enough loans to feed my family—as well as I hated every second of it mostly because of who I was working for.

My new job was taking care of slimy loan originators who were making a killing at the clients' expense. As agree, we needed to be paid for the job we did, but not excessively at the clients' expense.

What I was going through and who I was working for was a very real part of what was happening during this time. You could be paid quite well, and even to do a terrible job. It was the tail end of an era of uncontrolled earnings and buyer creditworthiness!

I knew I needed to do more with myself. I was miserable, and our bills were taking me under, fast! So, I decided to look for another opportunity. Upon learning of my leaving, my remote company dished out some serious frustration. I heard, "You are not good enough to be an LO," and, "I needed someone better anyway…" and so on.

Their reaction didn't bother me one bit, because, after all that time, I had found my worth! I realized that my boss' words were a direct reflection of his anger at me, leaving him, and I refused to be subjected to his behavior. I deserved to be happy and able to pay my bills.

It didn't take long for me to find another company that would hire me to work from home. I wanted to go back to originating loans. I knew that I could do the work from home as well. Before long, I found a company that would let me originate, and then I was closing loan after loan, but this time I was more educated and became a value to my clients. Loan officers now had to be licensed. This was done in an attempt to clean up the industry, and mine had just come in the mail!

I wasn't just a paper pusher; I was a dream maker.

Once you have a taste of what this business really is, it is hard to walk away from. Now, I was back to the direct client relationship I had been missing. During this time of my life, I enjoyed waking up again, and I was still able to process mortgages while I juggled my babies. I didn't mind the balance between my job and home life one bit.

The more loans I closed, the faster I had to work. Soon, I needed help to keep up. So, I called my best friend, my ride or die. She was already working in the business and was in a bad situation. I won't go into details, but I can tell you that my friend needed someone to show her the correct way to do this business. It didn't take much to train her, and then I had the best partner to assist me every day.

We worked in a loft out of my home, meaning we had no location to meet clients, but it never affected our business. We made it work by meeting people in their homes and had a ton of fun doing it. In fact, we still talk about the memories we made while working together.

When we stepped up our marketing game, we didn't realize that Facebook would soon become the most widespread referral network to date. Instead, we hand-stamped and licked envelopes the old-fashioned way.

As we really started to dive into marketing ourselves, the results were huge. Everyone was still trying to either buy or refinance. The restrictions on who qualified were much stricter, but business was still being done!

Back then, social media was just being introduced; I remember thinking it was silly. I couldn't have been more wrong. I can say now that social media completely changed how I did business and helped put me on the map!

During this phase of my career, every single day, I was fortunate enough to work side by side with my best friend. We laughed from the time she showed up in the morning until the time she left. I didn't travel anymore, and we were closing so many loans that I didn't need to worry about my bills. We had pulled it off. Together.

As fun as that time was for me, I knew the bottom would be falling out soon. Every news channel added fuel to the already large fire of what was happening in the industry. Talk circulated about how people were terrified to do anything like invest money, buy homes, and use banks. All of it was hyped by the media. It was my mission to close as many loans as I could before I was left scrambling again.

That's the thing about being commissioned. You always need to be consistent and on your game. Cell phones made this easier, but keep in mind that cell phones were not computers at this time; they were purely a means of communicating away from your home or office. Cell phones didn't get cool until much later in my career.

I was still fairly young at this point, and even though I have always been driven, I wasn't where I am today. My kids got older and started watching every little action I took in my life. When we hit rock bottom, they felt that, and when life was good, they felt that, too.

I was a little too young to fully understand what my life was destined for. I was just living in the moment and not really applying myself the way that I would in the future as my children grew. It is a funny thing what having kids can do for you. They saved my life. I never truly understood what motivation even looked like until I had my kids.

The desire to pick myself back up at my moment of weakness came from my kids. Having children taught me to care enough to be serious about my life.

As the industry crumbled, it wasn't fun anymore. It was stressful, and I didn't have the heart to move forward. I had just spent a great deal of my life investing in a career that disappeared before my eyes. I didn't have the strength to fight it. I had always been on point and up for a challenge, but I was completely done with the mortgage industry.

Those days became the darkest of my life. I completely jumped out of the mortgage business and started working for an insurance company. Even though I worked from home, I still worked midnights for the additional shift premium, and *why not*; I was a night owl. Despite those long hours, I made very little and had a little one by my side during the day.

I also had some rather large bills to pay because working as a processor for that short time had drained my savings.

It didn't take long for it all to hit our home hard. We barely hung on to our cars. We even pulled our four-year-old out of daycare to help offset the expenses. I was working every second of overtime that I possibly could to try to bring money in—only to remain behind, financially. It was the worst feeling in the world.

I can honestly say this was the hardest time in my life, and I was exhausted, falling asleep on my kid during the day. No matter how much overtime I worked, it was never enough to keep up with our bills. My husband was working by this time, but we lived a lifestyle that incurred the debt of an income we no longer had.

I spent three years begging to be promoted and getting nowhere with the insurance company. My nights were blending into the same routine every single day. I was so used to the chaos of originating loans and the deadlines to keep me on my feet. Night after night, it was the same calls and the same work, and I grew weary. I was earning a paycheck but not enjoying what I did and was still behind every single month.

Clearly, my job wasn't working for us. My refrigerator was empty; I had a budget of $40 a week to feed my kids and used every coupon I could find to pull that off. It was one more project for a tired momma. I could go to the store, buy in bulk and come out with $250-worth of stuff for $80 that would last almost until the end of the month. I learned very quickly how to budget with nothing to spare. We were always behind and playing catch up.

Facebook became a marketplace during this time, and I was selling almost every possession—including the clothes off my back. If you think that your kids are not watching you, remember this…they always are.

This would be one of the most talked-about times in our lives. My oldest still remembers it. I had completely given up on myself and lost my spark and confidence. It didn't get any easier from there, I am afraid.

After enduring so much financial hardship, everything changed one day in the worst way possible. I remember the day because it still haunts me. I relive it over and over and over again. I may have been down on myself at this point, but I had an amazing support system and no real reason to give up on my life.

What I would soon learn about someone I loved would change me forever and make me eternally grateful for what I had.

CHAPTER 6

DEATH MOVED ME

"Heaven is a place nearby, so there is no need to say goodbye." ~ Lene Marlin

Despite my hardships, I had some of the best nights out an overworked, tired momma could have. I used the strength of my friends to carry me through this time and was very grateful they were there to keep me sane.

We may not always like the circumstances we are in, but with good friends, it can be manageable.

We were ten girls with a bond dating back to high school that could not be broken. Or so we thought.

And we were a fearless bunch of incredible women—all of us different in many ways except one: the love that we had for each other. That love would grow as the years went on. We may not have had every day to spend together because life kept us all busy and running in different directions, but we still made time for Bunco night. It brought us all together.

I would be increasingly thankful for the time we made for each other before long because our lives were about to be impacted in a way that we would never recover from.

One evening, as I sat in my garage, I received a call that changed our group of friends forever.

I can still hear the voice of the nurse on the other line, choked up and devastated: "You need to come to the hospital right now. It's not good."

My best friends' sister and longtime friend was in trouble. Our desperate pleas for information from this nurse, who was also our friend, fell on deaf ears. We knew she wouldn't share a word because she was bound by her oath. Despite her silence, I knew instantly what we were going to find once we got to the hospital. I just couldn't bear to think about it.

In a panic, I raced to the hospital to find my friend lying lifeless on a bed. She was surrounded by her family as

I walked in to kiss her forehead for the last time. The sounds of the sobbing in her room will forever be stuck in my head. I won't forget the terrified look in her husband's eyes. Her usually tanned skin was pale, and the beautiful soul I loved so much was taken from her very body. There would be no more stories to look back on with her from this night on. No more belly laughs until you cry.

I was staring at my friend for the last time. Her sister, who is also my best friend, was broken. An accident had tragically taken away a sister, a mother, a daughter, and a friend far too soon.

Nothing in life prepares you for death. That hurt of losing someone you love radiates through your entire body. It's a sick feeling that won't go away. I needed to get some air. I couldn't be in that room any longer. It was filled with too many people and was so small that it felt like the walls were caving in.

Why did they have us in such a small room to tell her goodbye? Shouldn't they have known this room would have been crowded?

I remember seeing my friend's mother pull up to the hospital as I tried to catch my breath outside. She stopped her vehicle dead in the emergency parking zone, and, as she got out, she was greeted by her surviving daughter in one of the most horrific scenarios you could imagine. I watched her mom fall to her knees, wishing that what she was hearing was a dream—that this nightmare was not real. But it was.

Life isn't fair.

I am not even sure I really know the whole story about how she died, but to me, that is irrelevant. My friend Marie was gone, and she shouldn't have been. It didn't matter how. I would cherish every single one of the wild nights that we'd had, and we had a lot of them.

Now it was my time to be strong. All ten of us needed to step up to the plate to help this hurting family.

Without hesitation, everyone exchanged nights to help around her house so that her immediate family all had meals as her tribute to life was planned. We spent as much time as we could with her grieving family and offered up as many hugs as they needed. Kissing the tears away from her babies, explaining that she is gone, but will never be forgotten.

I spent a greater part of the timeframe after she died in a complete loss of my thoughts. I was left with the clear picture of the last time we had spent together, which was a recent wedding. I remember the dress she was so excited to wear, the peacock feather earrings dangling from her ears, and how she danced her heart out the whole night. I'd carried a snapshot of that moment with me every day and now I proudly display in my office the photograph that captured our last night out together.

She reminds me that life is short and to make the best out of every single moment.

I kept trying to find a way that I could have prevented her death and kept my friend here on Earth. I wanted to show up at the baseball fields and find her there. I would have given anything for one more football game sitting by her side. I couldn't change the outcome of what had happened, despite how badly I wanted to.

There would be no more late nights out with her crazy ass. This was the end of an era of friendship, and I just couldn't come to terms with it, but it wasn't just me who was hurting; her family was hurting. Our friend group was hurting. We had been left a scar that could not be erased.

We desperately tried to hold the group together for years after that and every time, the pain to see each other without her was just too much. So we opted not to get together for Bunco anymore. I didn't only lose my friend; we all fell apart without the glue of her persuasive personality.

I remember going to work in the days that followed her death and how I was completely numb. I remember being so proud of her for having life insurance even though she was young. I knew her family was going to be okay.

I was lost without her. And her loss helped me to see that I had no desire to return to my passionless and less-than-mediocre pay job.

The questions kept swirling in my head: *If something were to happen to me, could I afford another bill to carry the life insurance needed to protect my family?*

The answer was no and knowing that lit a fire under my ass to take my life back and get my shit together.

Marie's death moved me. It made me get off my ass and realize that sitting around moping and feeling sorry for myself was not the life that I wanted for myself. It made me realize that my children deserved a mother who would fight for them, and that meant providing a better life for them.

CHAPTER 7

THE SHOW MUST GO ON

"The question isn't who's going to let me… It's who's going to stop me." ~Ayn Rand

Every day after Marie's death was a challenge, but I let her spirit guide me on my quest to find myself. I wasn't sure what that entailed, but I was about to find out.

We had spent so much time together laughing over the years, getting into trouble no one ever knew about, and all of those memories came into my head at once.

That is why death is hard to process. It is hard to stop your heart when your head does not allow the proper time to heal. My head had every moment that we spent together on repeat. I needed something to take my mind off what my heart could no longer bear.

This was during the time when social media became a business tool, and when I started searching late at night for job opportunities that my connections and friends might know about.

One night, I noticed a post from a former boss seeking a mortgage loan processor, so I reached out. Even though he had let me go, it was worth a try to see where it might lead. I didn't let the fear of him brushing me off, stop me from attempting to give it another try.

Again, I was putting myself out there in the mortgage industry, learning a whole new game after three years of being out of the business. Since the collapse, the industry had completely changed. Even though the job I'd had remained the same, there was a whole new set of guidelines for loans that I needed to lock down.

What I was learning about was an entirely new job opportunity where I would be starting all over again. I didn't know if it was the right move, but that didn't stop me from discussing the opening.

There I was, broken after losing my friend, but I made myself a promise to choke down any fears that I had and run with it. I allowed myself to be back in the game and told myself I was truly meant for the industry; then I set up an interview.

Sometimes you need a hard slap in the face to set you back in the right direction, and the death of my best friend made me realize that I was spiraling out of control. The life I was living was not what my life was meant to be. I was bored out of my mind, and I needed to be challenged.

Our days are not promised, and I don't want to say that I'd lived a mediocre life because I was not born to be mediocre. The fact was that I had nothing to leave my children but debt if something happened to me. I wasn't even getting by. No, I was in a depression, but the tragedy of my friend's death awakened me.

I interviewed with the operations manager while wearing the same outfit and butterfly pin in my hair that I wore to say goodbye to my friend.

I had purposely chosen to do that so she could be with me as I embarked on this newest venture. I remember sitting in that office and being asked a ton of questions about my ability and where I thought my career might be headed by this gentleman and really liking him. He had a very calming nature and a fun spirit. If I was going to be reporting to someone, I was thankful it was him—especially in this moment of my life.

I didn't have the stamina to survive another cruel boss. And I knew some days in this industry would be a challenge, so having someone cool and compassionate on the other end was a must-have for me.

This time, I had way more experience under my belt and knew that I would not compromise working for someone who didn't value me. No longer would I allow anyone to control my happiness in the workplace. If that meant leaving ten jobs, then so be it. It just wasn't worth the damage being done.

I'd spent the last four years beating myself up; hearing every negative word management had preached at me year after year, and I'd realized no amount of money is worth the inner battle and the hard road to recovery.

I left the interview that day, thinking I had made the right decision to get back into mortgages, even if that job wasn't the one.

Still, I was going to continue on with my pursuit. I was feeling so much better about my life and where I was heading. I no longer felt the need to stay in pajamas all day and even wanted to put makeup on again. That particular time, leading up to that moment, was the hardest I had ever gone through. I had lost so much. Along the way, I had lost my dignity and my house and barely held onto my cars.

But not anymore. I was done losing and could see the fire again in my eyes when I looked in the mirror. For the first time in a very long time, I was awake.

I struggled for longer than I should have, but I didn't reach out for help either. I should have recognized the symptoms of depression and sought treatment, but I never did.

I'd wasted so much of my life being disappointed in myself. It was something that I could have solved with therapy had I made the effort. I've since learned how to value and love myself, but I've also started telling myself that I am worth it. If you have this mindset, that is all the motivation you need to get yourself out of bed in the morning.

I may have been broken but I was on my way to healing.

Shortly after I left the interview, I got the call offering me the processing position. The pay was better, but it was still not enough to build savings, and by the time I factored in my gas and the toll expense for the commute, I was probably losing money. The other downside was that I was back to traveling. Still, I knew I needed to start somewhere, and I also knew I would need to make compromises.

I had a lot of respect for the new director of mortgages anyway, but since I felt like I had been given a second chance, I had even more respect for him.

I worked as fast as I could to be the best at my new job. I refreshed myself on all of the updates and found my groove with my work once again.

It felt amazing.

I was back.

I no longer cried at night.

I no longer felt like I couldn't take care of my kids.

I knew I had a ways to go to get to where I wanted to be, but I found the strength to keep pushing forward.

I wouldn't stop until I reached my destination.

I am not sure if feeling this renewal of strength and purpose was due to my age or where I had been the last few years, but I would never again allow myself to wallow in my tears. That was behind me now.

I made some good friends at this new job and met a few people I could do without. The struggle of the juggle was real. I was missing so many parts of my kids' lives again, and I was reminded just how much of my life I had given up years ago.

What price was I to pay for working in this field?

But the grass isn't always greener on the other side; it is truly greener where you water it. Knowing this, I attempted to make the best of where I was working.

As I showed my strength in this position, I would get more and more piled on top of me from the director. Just when I thought I was finished, I quickly realized he would suck more out of me, and the way in which he did it stung.

He constantly played on my weaknesses. I am a perfectionist by nature, and when I made a mistake, it was already felt; I didn't need to be berated. Then like many victims experience, after the berating stopped, he told me how wonderful I was.

But because I had my courage again, I fought back, and ours became a tug-of-war relationship that resulted in me crying almost every single day.

I wasn't going fast enough; I'd made a mistake on this deal and on and on. It was exhausting being micromanaged. I was emotional, and healing from the loss of my friend, and this micromanaging was sending me right back from what I fought so hard to get away from: depression.

My boss made it seem like everything that went wrong was caused by me and that none of it was on him. After all, it is normal that you are pushed to a frustration level of tears every day by a boss, right?

Okay, so maybe I stayed in that position a little too long. I juggled my emotions and, at that time, felt as if I owed a favor to the person who'd given me an opportunity.

That was ridiculous! I didn't owe anyone besides myself. I am a people pleaser by nature, and it crushed me that I'd disappointed my boss. I wanted nothing more than for him to be proud of me. That day never came, despite all of my efforts.

No matter how fast I worked, I second-guessed myself because that is what happens when you are micromanaged and pushed to move faster than you should be moving. That is also when mistakes happen.

I caught myself working later and later and arriving home to spend less and less time with my family. *Just one more loan,* I would tell myself, *then the boss will back off.*

But one more loan would lead to one more loan. I was weak, and he played on that. He played into my lack of confidence better than I had ever seen anyone do, and I allowed it. I told myself that I had to take what he dished out to give my kids a better life. But the truth was, the pay was absolute crap; my self-esteem was crushed once again, and I was stuck.

No matter how much my husband would try to pull me up and tell me that I was capable of so much more than

I gave myself credit for, I wouldn't listen to him. I wouldn't listen to my friends or anyone else who knew me best. I had to believe the truth for myself, but at the moment, I didn't think I was worth more.

Thinking like this is what keeps us working for "the man." It's what holds us back. Fear drove me to that office every single day—fear of not making it without my job and fear of not providing for my children. I may have been able to dig myself out of depression, but I wasn't ready to remember how strong I was just yet.

So, I let my boss manipulate me. I let him talk down to me. I made endless lunchtime phone calls to friends to talk me down off the ledge. There were countless interventions by the operations manager, and we would end up right back in the same place. I was tired of being talked down to and had had enough.

My boss only controlled my happiness because I allowed him to, but I am no longer that victim. I promised myself that I would never allow it again.

The catch was that I was no longer the woman who was lacking knowledge of her worth. And this moment is one I wouldn't take back. I made some great friends along the way while I worked at that company. But above all, it made me stronger. It made me realize what I didn't want to tolerate from anyone ever again. I refuse to ever let anyone treat me like I am worthless.

Working at that company was a great test and one that I needed so I could step out of the funk I was in.

Sometimes we need to hit bottom so that we can appreciate the climb back to the top.

The day came when I realized that I was not about to waste any more of my time in that position. I had saved every single penny during my time as a processor. It wasn't enough. I had tried to prove myself as a staple in the company, time and time again, with the hopes that it would pay off in a big way. But the effort was not enough. It had to be okay anyway.

The longer the head of the department pushed me down, the angrier I became. I didn't want to leave the place that I was working for, and I reminded myself that the reason I'd gone for this job was to give myself a refresher, notate the business changes and then segue back into a loan officer position.

Being on the operations side comes with a salary and consistency, but it lacks what I desire most—being close to home and working with clients directly. It was fine to live off commission when I was younger, but I was in debt up to my eyeballs by now.

My situation continued to deteriorate at work, and I was being pushed to take a stand.

I approached the sales director with the request to go back to sales. At that time, none of the employees worked from home, but I intended to change that. The sales team all worked inside the branch.

I needed to spread my wings and fly and was confident that the growth of social media could put me on the map. I was fascinated by the marketing aspect of the job and had some big ideas on how I could throw myself directly into the audience that was my home community.

My employer went for it!

They agreed I could take on the sales role and make the change from loan originating. I wouldn't have stayed if the result had been different because I was on a mission to use social media to build my client base and to allow myself time with my children through the remote position.

I worked tirelessly day in and day out, building my book of business on social medial. The sicker to my stomach I felt about needing money and switching back to a commissioned job, the harder I worked. I would not get derailed by the need for a salary. Feeling terrified, I marketed on social media like a madwoman. Multiple times a day, my name would pop up in front of homeowners. In addition to working general social media, I launched a group specific to homebuying in my county—the first one I had seen in the state. That big idea would prove to be extremely crucial in building what I have today.

The good thing about being a commissioned employee is that you don't have a cap on your income. Now, it's true there is a very real chance of failing, but I believe the reason people fail is that they give up on themselves.

My children were watching my every move. They deserved a mother who wouldn't give up on them.

Since I had spent a great portion of the last few years finding a way to make it without having much money, I learned how to prolong the savings that I did have for six months before I saw the payoff and actually brought in a paycheck. Not too bad for a momma making moves on the fly!

The best part of the situation was that I was working from home, completely separated from the travel. My new position also changed my relationship with the director. I was now in a position that allowed me to distance myself from management, which proved to be a huge success.

CHAPTER 8

THE RISE OF BEAUTIFUL ME

"There is no force more powerful than a woman determined to rise."
~Dorothy Dandridge

How hard is waking up in the morning and telling yourself that you are capable of anything you set your mind to?

It's very hard, but that doesn't mean it's impossible.

You just have to love yourself.

If there is one thing that I can take away from my lifetime so far, it is that I am proud of who I have become and just how hard it was to get here. I am proud of overcoming the struggles I faced. I am even proud of the failure.

Nothing changed until I had the mindset to change. I started off every single morning, reminding myself that I was capable of anything. Changing my mindset helped me reach success, which has resulted in a happy lifestyle.

I traded negative-minded friends on social medial for those who motivate me. Staying high energy and in touch with positive influences helped encourage me along the way, too. That is the thing about social media. You can add or cut out anyone, and I chose to remove all the negativity.

Every single morning, I am greeted by a host of individuals out there living their best life. The power of reading a post that inspires you or hearing a podcast that encourages you to be your best can really help retrain your mind. And you need to get your mind right, so you can grind right. So let go of those who drag you down.

You can choose to spend your day scrolling through a bunch of political-filled hate, constant complaining, or dealing with the lurkers—you know, the ones who like your post from eight years ago by "accident"? Or, you can choose to build your network based around the people who inspire you to be better than you were yesterday. Those are my people.

Six months in at my new job, my social media game was taking shape. It took relentless effort day and night to find ways of self-promotion. I was dealing with a completely different market now. The days of finding business in a call center environment, sending mailers, and traditional marketing were not working anymore. Those methods were long gone.

We had grown into a society of instant results. People wanted easy online shopping, and I was determined to use social media as my platform. To do that, I needed to create an audience and set myself apart from the rest. I wanted to create my own brand. Branding myself allowed me to never rely on a company name. I would rely on my own.

Doing this was completely outside of my comfort zone—as I am not a huge fan of doing videos—but time and time again, video has proven to be a consistent organic method of showing your knowledge to potential clients.

The pressure was on to distinguish myself in my home community, but the people were less than inviting. I couldn't let that get to me. I also know that we are our worst critics. If a 12-year-old child could gain wealth playing video games, I could most certainly find a way to capture an audience for the purpose of educating future home buyers. Without having a client base and much of a savings, I had to figure it out as fast as possible.

I put a plan into place, and, before long, bit by bit, gained traction—enough to make a name for myself. Knowing how to underwrite and process a loan had finally paid off.

Right about this time, I was introduced to a company that would change my life and how I felt about the business in general.

I had noticed a strange gentleman in my office being entertained by my boss, and I wondered if he was ever going to introduce me. It had been a few hours that the man was there and no introduction yet. That's how informed my boss kept me.

As it turns out, I had been on the longest interview of my lifetime because this person happened to be at my office to hash out the details of my new position and company. I wasn't involved in the meetings and wondered what was discussed prior to me being introduced.

Rather than make a scene, I figured I would connect with this person and discuss what he wanted afterward. I assumed the conversation would revolve around a new opportunity, and I was right. We had discussed me running my own branch, and I heard it mentioned as "in the works."

Well, I think we all have our own definition of "in the works," and it is subject to whom is speaking that term. I kind of passed it off and went back to work. I most certainly did not expect that opportunity to have come so soon.

I was beyond excited. Not only was I getting my own branch, but I was going to work close to home at a time in my boys' lives where they really needed me to be there. They were growing up fast, and the sports they were in became even more difficult for one parent to manage.

Finally, all the time I had invested in the industry had paid off. I couldn't have been happier.

This was a monumental moment in time for me, and the coming months would engage me on levels that I never imagined.

I will never forget the chaos of the day as I set up my new office. We dived into opportunities: this new branch, marketing, ribbon cuttings, and parties. *Someone, please pinch me. Is this really happening?*

Meeting Jack (the man who had been hanging around my boss' office) was huge for me. He finally understood my vision. He not only shared the same social media vision as me, but he also happened to be the senior vice president of a growing mortgage company—which would eventually prove to be an amazing opportunity.

Even though I had no clue why I was meeting Jack that day, we engaged in conversation about expanding what I had been building on and organic marketing— things that my current boss hadn't explored and couldn't relate to. Finally I felt as if I was where I was meant to be with a company. It was official; I had the location now, and I was moving to a new company while I did it.

No matter how slow of a ride it was to get here, I wouldn't change a thing about my career.

One day, I was interviewing loan officers and chatting about opportunities for the branch; my day was packed. One of my interviews was a lifelong friend in the industry and a loan officer. I adored her but knew that her heart wasn't in it anymore (btw, I was right, as she is now teaching). Maybe I gave her a little nudge to focus on her dream, maybe not, but for her, it was the right decision.

I was also preparing a new loan officer to get licensed. She was passionate about helping the people that I had hired. In this business, we may be doing the same thing, but most people have a different background and approach to business than we do.

For example, someone who has been on the job for fifteen years is probably dead set in their ways, and that might not align with your business plan. If they were against social media, that was not the path that I wanted for my team. They wouldn't make a great fit. I wanted to make sure whoever was hired shared the same goals for growing the company as me.

Being so close to home was an absolute dream for me. I felt I had been preparing for that my entire career— no more three-hour-a-day commutes. Time with my kids had been few and far between over the course of the last year, and I was determined to change that. I wanted to be closer to my children. They were growing up before my eyes, and I had missed so much over the years. I simply couldn't be an absent parent anymore, but I also didn't want to give up my job.

I had some serious time invested in getting the building ready to open. I had been working all day long while juggling the kids, followed by my hubby and I spending our nights gathering building supplies and working on a build for the new office. I wanted so badly to prove to my husband that I was going to crush this. I was not going to let anything stop me. My husband's unwavering support made the transition so much easier, and the long nights worth it.

Anyone can be offered an opportunity, but it is up to you to decide if you will make the most of it or let it pass you by. I had wasted enough of my time and knew that no matter what obstacle I faced; I was prepared. I wasn't going to run away. I was going to find a way to live up to the potential I had. I made a promise to hold myself accountable for my actions and to not piss away money as I had when I was an irresponsible young mother.

This was a chance to change my life and help my children and some amazing people along the way.

No greater feeling exists for me in the workplace than helping people achieve what they thought was never possible. Through this new office, our clients were being given the gift of the American dream. They had the opportunity to be homeowners.

My newest loan officer shared the same desire. She is the complete opposite of me, and I have found having this trait is crucial when you hire someone. You will always need a different perspective and someone who will complement the areas of your business that are missing.

No matter who we are, we have areas of strength and weakness. Being a great manager is knowing what those are so that you can develop a plan to overcome them. Being a leader means you are someone who demonstrates what is possible.

I knew that this loan officer was going to be a rising star. She came into the job with no experience at all—which I prefer. I would rather train someone than retrain them.

I wanted to provide a less panicked and more educated approach when it came time to selecting which financing option was better for the client. In earlier years, very few loan programs and guidelines clearly printed what they would allow. But lending had changed over the years. Qualifying became stricter, but that also made sense, given the mess we had come out of with the earlier crash. I didn't want my clients to feel anything but encouraged and supported when they closed on their homes. When it comes to closing a loan, it is never easy, but it is always worth it.

In this new location, I wanted to focus my attention on first-time buyers. I was going to lead them toward their dreams and show them that owning a home was possible.

After all, I am living proof that dreams do come true with enough hard work. Just four years before, I didn't have anything and lacked a reason to even get up in the morning.

Now I knew I had the power to encourage others because I had been there and experienced such pain. I wasn't any different than anyone else struggling. I was the girl who had messed up her credit, the girl who had lost her home, and the girl who had given up on herself and her dreams. Then my mission changed. I encouraged others to live their dreams.

The business opened in my hometown, and I was in my element. I continued to work day in and day out, pushing social media as a means of creating referrals.

My strategy for growing my business was working exactly as I had planned. I'd wanted to grow my business and steadily close more loans. And I was doing all of those things.

I consistently posted on social media three times a day, and this put the spotlight on me in my friend list. It made me a recognizable name. I kept on promoting myself in the group I had created and other similar groups. The art of using social media to grow my business was only the beginning of where my marking would lead to!

CHAPTER 9

CUTTING TOXICITY

"Letting go of toxic people is an act of self-care." ~Karen Salmansohn

I completely absorbed all the advice that branch managers within this new company offered. I felt like I was home. They lit a fire under me by example, by their marketing ideas and collective collaborations. By everything they did and represented. They were so eager to share success stories, and they really took me under their wings.

Working with them was extraordinary, and unlike anything I had ever experienced. As time went on, we became family. In this company, I found what I had been missing for so very long. Across the country, each branch became each other's social network supporters, and if you think that doesn't matter in business, you are mistaken. It is crucial to have a team that supports you on social media. People are always watching. Even if they do not like or comment, they are always watching your every move. This is why having back up is necessary and why if you don't have it, your posts will get less attention. They were and still are my tribe.

I was no longer locking bullhorns with one specific manager. In fact, I didn't have much contact with him at all. I didn't separate from the employment and was still technically intertwined as he claimed a title over me, which limited my control. So, I wasn't really a branch manager. I carried the license.

"Branch Manager" was more of a title than the role. I had no control over this branch, and it became clear just how little control I actually did have. I was a face and a nameplate—a puppet.

I might have been part of the team, but my branch was not experiencing what the other branches were going through in building together. Because of that, I felt as if I were controlled and as if my potential was limited.

Here I had co-workers across the county who were teaching me how to run a business and manage profit and loss, and expenses, and so on, and I couldn't even see expenses. My arrangement as a branch manager was far different from other branch managers, but I didn't complain about it until it affected my everyday working environment. Since I had no control and no clue what was going on, it was apparent that my branch was being mismanaged. I felt the effects of that. Rent wasn't being paid, and I was looked at for the solution.

That was it! It was time to go off on my own and cut the ties with my boss. It was long overdue. For some time now, I had questioned so much, and I wasn't wrong. I was no one's puppet, and I wanted the chance that I had been promised—to have my own branch.

I'd felt for so long that I'd owed my boss. When he'd hired me, I had been grieving the loss of a friend. He'd given me the opportunity to get my feet wet again. But now I was not worth the control of the branch amid the worry over mismanagement. I know this was not the case; it wasn't that I wasn't ready; it was control.

Yet I had built up far too much to let my career slip away. I was finally on my way to a steady and level business. But now was the time. If the rent wasn't being paid, what else was coming down the road for me?

Surviving that wave in my career and family life was excruciating, but it also paved the way for me to get to where I am today. So I have no regrets.

Only one possible situation would benefit me. I had to stay put and sever ties with my boss, and I had to do it as soon as possible. Without doing so, I would never have my opportunity. But I needed to keep my current branch and the company I was working for.

Since I was already scheduled to meet the corporate office, other branches, and the staff in Texas, the timing was perfect to ask them if they would take me on without my boss and keep the branch going.

Without any spare cash to my name, I will never forget being driven to the airport by my father, who handed me his last forty dollars. He couldn't afford to give me the cash either as work had been slow for him. But he did it for me anyway.

I had never been to Texas, and all I remember was how hot it was. Landing in Houston was muggy. Coming from Chicago felt as if I had been greeted by a free facial just for stepping outside the airport.

I took in the scenery as I waited outside to be joined by yet another branch manager who would attend the meetings we were about to have. So far, I was holding on to that original forty dollars my dad had given me. I didn't spend a penny of it. My ride in, plane, and hotel room were all covered.

I didn't know it then, but this trip would become a yearly thing for me, a time I would look forward to each year. My co-workers and I formed relationships at these in-person meetups. I cherished them.

Throughout the course of the next few days, the branches got together to discuss business, creative strategies, and our plans for growth and development. This meeting was run differently than anything I had seen in my career. The message was about what support they could offer us and letting us be the deciding factor in business moves on the horizon. I wasn't quite sure how to react, but I know my smile probably said all that needed to be said.

When the meetings over the next few days had ended, we spent time getting to know each other, and I remember looking in my purse at the forty dollars and knowing that I was returning home with the clarity of where I wanted to be. Before I left, I spoke with the senior vice president and explained the situation with the rent and the uncertainty that I faced back home. I asked him for a chance to prove that I was capable of managing the branch on my own. He admitted sometime later that he had called me down to the meeting for that very reason.

As I look back, I can see that we were trying to see if my branch and I would be a good fit. I further explained to the senior vice president that I knew the money for the rent was there because I was closing the loans to cover the cost. It just wasn't being paid. And I assured the senior vice president that I had a great game plan for our growth. I knew that I could handle it.

This is one of my most favorite career moments. I looked the senior vice president in the face as I talked to him about what I needed, and thought should be done. When I was finished talking, without hesitation, he replied: "Done." He also asked me if I wanted to cut ties with my director, and I politely refused, saying, "It's my problem to solve." I needed to rip off that Band-Aid and separate from what had caused me agony over the years. I needed to stand up and use my voice. Yes, my boss had given me an opportunity, but that did not mean it was a prison sentence.

Meeting everyone from that company really sealed the deal for me. They were so welcoming and made me feel at home while I was in Texas. I must admit it was hard to return home. We all bonded so well.

Every single moment in my life has made me who I am, and attending this meeting was no exception. And even though I had been terrified of asking for control over my branch, I refused to let fear stop me.

I remember being a kid, and seeing my parents earn a living while they were raising us kids. They made it look easy. I watched my mom and dad run a business, but we never talked much about that, although we lived a great life. I just always assumed they did quite well, and when you are younger, you don't pay money much attention. All I knew was that they were always home by early evening to be with the family. My mother had some flexibility in her job, and they were both very present in our lives. I assumed their lives were easy, but now I know that assumption couldn't have been farther from the truth. Adulthood is not easy and running a business was not easy for them, but they shielded us from that pretty well.

My parents divorced after thirty years of marriage, and I have a feeling their working relationship in the business might have led to some of the pain points in their marriage. I know I speak for myself when I say, sometimes separation from your spouse is great. I also know that that aspect of their lives was only a portion of the truth for them. Sometimes it just doesn't work out, and that is okay, too.

Thinking that I had it all figured out, I was a young, bright-eyed girl, envisioning all my hopes and dreams in the most naive of ways. That proved to be a fairytale. I didn't become the attorney I had planned on being. As I worked to build my career and struggled through credit challenges, I fell on my face. I know now I needed to fall on my face to learn what I wanted to do with my life.

My failures taught me how strong I really was, and that strength allowed me to break free of toxic people surrounding me. Some of these people were from my social network; some were employers, mentors, and some even came from my family. Cutting out some of these people was painful, but it was necessary for me to move forward. As I examined who was in my life, I placed boundaries on how much I allowed myself to be influenced by others, and I only allowed people to be close to me if they inspired me.

I dismissed negativity and opted for self-awareness and accountability for my actions instead.

It's a very powerful and pivotal turning point when you distance yourself from pain and hold yourself accountable. It is acceptable to let go of toxicity. The result is overwhelmingly freeing.

I dove into my career with fearless passion when I returned home from that meeting.

It took me four long years to recognize that my talents were not meant for anything else but what I was doing, that I was born to use my powerful personality and pushy tendencies for the greater good of helping others.

I will never get the time back from all of my travels leading up to this point, but I made sure my children's diaries weren't filled with stories of how their mother had failed in life and simply gave up. That would not be the case.

Ladies, if you are crying because of the way management is treating you, stand your fucking ground. Do not let anyone compromise your sense of security, and most importantly, do not wait as long as I did to come to terms with it. I spent three years being punished. Ripping off that Band-Aid never felt so good. I was free.

I grew up this way and felt as though this treatment was something normal. But clearly, these were my issues. I was letting someone else determine how I felt about myself.

A good boss can make you perform to the best of your ability; a bad boss can leave scars.

Marketing myself relentlessly on social media was paying off in a big way. I had made a name for myself as a reliable source of information in my field in the very community where I lived. The best advocates were my previous clients, and they still are today. They are the first to tag me in a post when someone is looking for a recommendation. They freely share their experiences.

Social media was as I had predicted it would be all of those years ago—a game-changer for doing business.

I am a better manager because I have seen the damaging effects of bad management. Every wrong way to run a business has been checked off my list. And all my failures have been justified because I learned what not to do in the future as I came to believe that I am capable of whatever I set my mind to! I learned to love myself and all my strange flaws. I am my own beautiful self, and so are you.

I tell you my story because I am not alone. Someone out there is in the same situation. If it is you or someone you know, I want to help in the way that I was helped.

End the toxicity.

Ever since I found my way back to being the person I was always meant to be, I have made it my mission to encourage others to keep fighting for themselves.

I always start off every single day with encouragement. I tell myself that I am capable and worth it. And I share this on my social media, where I get messages from others thanking me for the encouragement I share. My posts have helped people in ways I could never have imagined. I've learned I have empowered people to start living the dream they have been putting off—that watching me live my dream has encouraged others to live theirs. I know that I am right where I am supposed to be and am forever grateful to the people who have helped shape my life.

Thank you.

CHAPTER 10

FLYING HIGH

"Refuse to be average. Let you heart soar as high as it will." ~A.W. Tozer

My ultimate plan was in place. I was going to build my dream, the way that I wanted, with full control. Not only was I able to maintain the business; I made it thrive. An overwhelming sense of satisfaction came along with that. I no longer had a hand on my head, holding me back. I wasn't incapable. I just hadn't been offered the opportunity to shine.

Liberating might be an understatement.

I went from making no money to taking control of my life. With my control of the business side, financial freedom soon followed.

The one good aspect of having no money is that the years of living off no money train you to budget a profit and loss every single month. When I have trained other branch managers, I tell them the same thing. Running a branch is like having a bigger checking account than your personal account, but the same bills. Balancing is crucial and spending within your means is how you optimize that.

My branch was a smaller unit, which helped us reduce out-of-pocket expenses for the business, but we were growing out of that space. It was a beautiful thing to see because it meant we had record-breaking months as we remained a constant in our community while providing solid advice and offering guidance to those who needed us.

Every single moment in our lives leads us to where we are meant to be. Without those financial struggles, I wouldn't have been ready to budget a business on a much larger scale. The struggles I'd faced in my life were worth it. Not giving up on myself enabled me to build my professional career in ways that I never imagined were possible.

This is why I encourage you to now more than ever, use the social media tools that are at your disposal and brand yourself. It doesn't matter the size of your business.

You will also want to find your tribe of like-minded support. This may include personal acquaintances who follow and support your goals, or it might be business professionals. Support is crucial as you grow on social media and in your business, and I am thankful for the team I have in place.

We meet people for a reason. I refuse to see the relationships I've had as anything else. I don't suffer from regret. Not everyone that we come across in the workplace will have your best interest at heart. Some will see you as a paycheck; some will see you standing in their way; some will even be ruthless and cold, and that is okay. The right employers are out there. Keep searching until you find them.

When I made this major change in my business to stay with the same company and separate myself from my boss, I was no longer pushed into doing tasks that I was not comfortable with. I wasn't told that I was horrible. In fact, I was loved and appreciated for who I was. I was no longer micromanaged. I was set free to be my beautiful self.

I know there is no one way to do business right because we are all very different people, but I can tell you that I have found bits and pieces of a working strategy because I was looking for it. I never claimed to know everything and having that attitude has helped me open my eyes to alternative ways of doing business. Sometimes even the slightest shift in what you are doing can become the last missing piece you have been waiting for. It may be something as small as creating video content when you are scared, or it might involve a larger scale concerning your business model. If you do something to make those changes, the results will come.

One year, I attended a mastermind event in Las Vegas and was bored by day two. On stage were supposed to be the greatest minds in the industry, inspiring me. The truth is, my peers and I had already implemented what was being taught, and we weren't following a crowd; we were leading it.

When you are in a room with powerful thinkers, you come out with more golden nuggets than you can envision. That is how the new company and I rolled as a team. We were one family made up of branch managers across the country.

Being teamed up with a work family, trading ideas, holding each other accountable, and building each other up is our company's mission. At other employers, you might expect feast or famine. I wouldn't trade what I have for millions of dollars.

At this time of my life, I was no longer struggling. My bare refrigerator was a thing of the past, and my confidence was back.

After one year of taking over the branch, I had tripled my income.

CHAPTER 11

STAYING CONSISTENT AND MOTIVATED

"If my strength intimidates you, I hope you realize that's a weakness of yours."
~Some awesome woman probably

I am not going to tell you that life is easy or that building a business has been a blast every single day because that wouldn't be the truth. I am, however, grateful.

I am not going to pretend that it didn't involve extreme sacrifices to my family, but I will tell you that they trusted in my vision even when I couldn't see it myself.

The support of your loved ones is crucial. If your circle is small, make sure those you engage with are worthy of your time and are inspiring you to be the best version of yourself.

It takes working just a little bit harder each day when you think you have nothing left to give. I assure you; you can always find a little more strength. You need to sacrifice your time now for the sake of eventual triumph.

My method is simple. I work until I am done. I do not leave emails unread, and I do not leave phone calls unanswered. I never ever leave my clients feeling like they don't matter to me because without them, I am unemployed.

We need to truly understand we have the pleasure of serving our clients. I work endless hours for the sake of others and understand that not everyone can push aside their emotions due to the weekend approaching.

Our work should never be a burden. If this is how you feel about your job, this is an opportunity for you to reflect on making a career change or to reevaluate yourself and your negative outlook.

I am driven by a passion to educate and gain a true understanding of how someone else relates to pressure. I feel compelled to perceive the apprehension they might be feeling and negate it by being the calming voice of reason. That is what I take comfort in and what gets me through each day.

Anyone can do what I do for a living, but no one can be me.

This is what I pride myself on and what has continued to allow me to build client relationships. I also take pride in the fact that I am genuine and true to my word.

When you feel like you are overwhelmed, you probably are. Make sure to constantly evaluate yourself and how you are running during each stage of your growth. Growing is immensely difficult, and when you start to feel growing pains, it's time to delegate responsibility. Some of the pressures need to come off you. You are not going to be your best if you are overwhelmed.

Delegating is extremely difficult for me, even now, and I have to take a step back to truly see that I am preventing my growth by not allowing others to step in and help me when I need an extra set of hands. We get so comfortable handling everything that we forget, asking for help is okay and necessary.

We all have specific areas where we are weak and some areas in which we dominate. If you are looking for ways to delegate your time to help you grow, you need to identify which tasks align with your strong side and focus your time and energy on those while handing off other tasks to someone who has strengths in areas you do not possess. If that person doesn't exist within your organization, then you must hire out to fill that spot. It is imperative that you keep your focus on what drives results based on your skillset.

I have an insane ambition that keeps me moving toward higher goals. I will probably never be satisfied, but that keeps me pressing ahead. And just like anyone else, I have both a comfort and a discomfort zone. My discomfort zone surrounds a fear of video. But if you follow me on social media, you will see that I do a ton of videos. It most certainly is not because I like to do them; it is because the information that I am sharing with others is important while my fears are less important. Besides, it is quite liberating to put yourself out there despite how terrified you are. The reward of surpassing those fears is imminent. I had to change the way that I was trained to think to do these videos.

When I started in my business, it was very much a hands-on situation, with the telephone connected to your ear and dialing consistently until you sold your quota. That is simply not how business is done today in sales. It involves so much more than that.

Business involves marketing and strategizing for a society that has become accustomed to instant results. The days of massive advertising costs are over. The phonebook has been replaced with organic network marketing, and our voices are heard on a much larger platform by countless individuals. In the case of media evolving, it can be hard to keep up, but this is necessary if you wish to stay relevant.

Social media has expanded our captive audience. There is no more shaking hands or buying lunches in the hopes that some real estate agent will give you the time of day and a shot at one of their clients. I can now bypass those old ways and speak directly to their clients. I can educate people about program advantages without involving any agents. That is how you get past the gatekeeper!

To stay ahead of the game, I continued to push myself. I came to terms with the fact that it wasn't going to hurt me to do videos. I was the only one who hated watching them. To this day, I don't ever watch the videos that I put out, and that is okay. Not everyone loves hearing themselves talk. But the results of doing those videos absolutely blew my mind. They didn't just get a little traction on social media; they put me on the map. Despite how much I dreaded doing them, they gave me instant results, which fueled my passion for marketing even more.

The key to social media marketing is engagement. Staying relevant on social media requires work, just like anything else you do, but if you do it effectively and consistently, you will be successful.

If I don't get a grip on my irrational fears, I will ridicule myself until I talk myself right out of it. I do not like the sound of my voice; I don't like my hair, and I pick on myself for my weight. But the sooner you stop worrying about what other people think of you, the more successful you will be. The true test is loving who you are in spite of all of your imperfections and critics. Success comes when you push yourself to continue on despite anything else.

Marketing is essential, and it needs to be done effectively. You need to fine-tune your audience.

When I am creating content for my next video or post, I consider who I want to reach and what my goals are in the message I am trying to create. Then I focus on the value they need, not what I want. You have to consider your approach and not just post content for the sake of posting content. I have tailored my social media presence to people who share the same goals as I do. If I have not interacted with someone or they are providing me no real value, then I have no point in keeping them in my network. It is truly that simple.

When you are assessing your social media network, ask yourself, *is this person providing me any value?* If not, it is okay to walk away from them. There is no shame in restructuring your profile to encompass a like-minded following. In fact, I encourage it!

Do you have any nay-sayers on social media? Get rid of them. Not only does it break your spirits, seeing negativity all the time, but the types of interactions that come from negative people are less than helpful as you grow. Negative Nancys need to go somewhere, but not in your network. Cut the cord, even if it is someone you love. If you want to build a business and you are following someone who inspires you, it is easy to put your best foot forward. Those are your people.

Find peace with who you are and live your dream. I am living proof of what can happen if you believe in yourself and allow yourself to push past your fears. Trust me, the people who are going to hate the videos you put out are the same people who secretly hated you anyway. Your video isn't going to change their idea of you. So, who gives a shit? Be your own beautiful self!

CHAPTER 12

A FINAL MESSAGE TO ALL THOSE WHO STRUGGLE

"Optimism is the faith that leads us to achievement." ~Helen Keller

We Are Women

Oftentimes, our value and self-worth are derived from the source that is feeding it, such as your employer, friends, and/or family. Make no mistake, it is great to be loved, but loving yourself despite the value placed upon you by others is liberating.

We tend to gravitate toward those who feed our soul with encouragement, love, and inspiration. When you combine fearlessness with self-worth, the desire to succeed, and a passion for inspiring minds, you set your career on fire. As quickly as you made the determination to change your outlook, you have changed your life.

What if you became the voice so many needed to hear? What if, instead of using social media as an outlet to rant, we turned it into strength by influence?

The level of support that I have witnessed over the last few years with women connected to me on social media is incredible. I have received messages from others that prove people are listening. Some of the messages included how I had inspired them to pursue their career goals or made them feel better during uncertain times in their lives. I have never met most of these women, but I can honestly say that we share the same views and goals. These women keep me motivated and inspired, and I have the power to do the same for them. We have been given a platform to help each other, and the results are unimaginable.

The power of a positive mindset alone will allow you to conquer your fears. When we put ourselves out in the public eye for everyone to see our flaws and imperfections, it can be scary.

You will have growing pains and missteps, but you will overcome those. Nothing of value comes from within your comfort zone. If I can move outside my comfort zone, so can you.

So, what if we valued our worth just a little bit more? Ask yourself where you plan to be in a year and start planning for a new approach. Goals are meant to slayed. We all have hopes and desires, and it is time to stop making excuses for why you cannot start now.

Excuses are dream crushers, not your circumstances. Most of the successful people that I have known in my life have shared one amazing thing—they fought their way to success. It wasn't handed to them. Most of them had arduous obstacles in life to overcome. You don't need to be the smartest in your field. As the saying goes, "Hustle beats talent when talent doesn't hustle."

Never fear the opinions of those around you, as they are inconsequential. I do not want to diminish the existence of the nay-sayers, skeptics, or critics, as they are quite important in helping provide motivation. But the more powerful your voice becomes the softer their whispers. Give no regard to them and stand strong in your convictions as these kinds of people cannot hurt you if you do not pay them any mind. Yes, understand the damage they can do if you let them. They can derail you if allowed, but also remember that combatting adversity is how we cultivate prosperity.

We Are Mothers

Having children is unlike anything that I have ever experienced. It is absolute insanity at times, but it is worth every single second. As your children grow, it becomes less complicated and less demanding because they become more independent. That doesn't mean that raising them becomes effortless; it just means your name is screamed less and less for endless snacks, butt wiping, and drink refills. It also means as they become older, there are fewer snuggles.

That was the part that I had the hardest time with as my children grew. I still miss being embraced by them. I used to be so sad when they were sick and only wanted to be loved. Now, they have grown into their own and are far past the days of needing me for every little thing. That sting in your heart is bittersweet.

As much as I would like to say that I enjoy them now that they are teenagers, I am compelled to share with you that it becomes quite a different lifestyle that you lead when that happens.

Maybe they no longer play sports, maybe the Chutes and Ladders game is thrown away, maybe you feel like you are losing them. When your kids grow up, it can be a very overwhelming change, especially if you are wrapped up in them. As much as it pained me years ago when I would travel all the time, and as much blame as I placed on myself for the time that was not spent, I needed to work.

Maybe it wasn't ideal back then, but if I had never taken that mortgage job in the suburbs years ago, I wouldn't be where I am today with my career, and the thought of that makes me ill.

I often ask myself why I punished myself by having a guilty conscience all those years when I worked because the reality is my children are independent and capable. They do not love me any less for working.

In understanding that we are mothers constantly juggling a balance between work and family, we also need to understand that we have our own needs as well. It is okay to desire and fulfill those needs without compromising your children's childhood.

My youngest one doesn't even remember the amount of time that I spent away from home, and if he did, all it would have shown him is how life sometimes is never perfect, but we just do the best we can. If I didn't have my career to fall back on now as they are older, I would be crawling out of my skin with boredom.

But I am not. Instead, I am thriving at work, and I now have more time to invest in myself because my kids need me less and less. That chapter is closing, and if I hadn't found my purpose back then, I would be wrestling emotions now over not knowing what to do with myself. I would have found it quite difficult to come to terms with the fact that I am no longer needed by my children.

I no longer feel like I was a bad mother. Instead, I feel like I prepared myself quite well for life's transition. I set out to do exactly as intended—raising self-determined, individualistic, self-supporting children. My reward for that is peace of mind and a career that I love.

For all of you struggling mothers out there, I will leave you with this. This is my story about hardships, survival, purpose, and triumph. Keep in mind that your hesitation is only going to delay your inevitable progress, and we have little minds to engage. Our children will ultimately mimic our efforts. We have given so much to them already; it is okay to resume who we once were. They will be inspired by our accomplishments in spite of our fears.

Loving our children is a part of who we are as nurturing women, but it doesn't have to be all that we are.

ACKNOWLEDGMENTS

To my mother, who never finished her book, I hope you see this as the best compliment ever as I followed your lead and wrote this for the both of us.

To my sisterhood of friends who have been by my side since high school, thank you for pushing me and guiding me every step of the way. Your encouragement and love are what keeps me whole.

To my brother, a writer himself, thank you for always seeing the best in me, even when I lost sight.

To my boys, Maycen and Madden, may this book serve as motivation for you to achieve your own personal goals, whatever they may be.

My husband, rock, and my lover, you complete me, and this book is only possible because I had you by my side.

ABOUT THE AUTHOR

Kelly Rice lives in Bourbonnais, Illinois, with her husband and two children. She is a wife, a mother, a ball buster, a writer, a dreamer, and is on a mission to fuel what sets her soul on fire.

A visionary in marketing, she developed and maintains a network of like-minded professionals and has built a successful platform using social media that encourages complete organic marketing in business.

As a mortgage loan originator, she was recognized in *National Mortgage Professional Magazine* as a leader in the industry, claiming the title of "Most Powerful

Woman" two years running, and yet another honor in 2019 when she was voted "Top 40 Under 40" in her profession.

Her passion and commitment to her team led her to grow a business, but her perseverance makes her a force to be reckoned with. Often labeled as the local "Bulldog" in business, she is responsible for helping her community achieve the dream of homeownership.

When she is not running a demanding business, you will find her surrounded by the ones she loves doing whatever it is she desires. Usually, that involves some type of shenanigans as she has a hard time sitting still, which remains a crucial part of her success story. A relentless drive to succeed navigates her every move.

www.ingramcontent.com/pod-product-compliance
Lightning Source LLC
Chambersburg PA
CBHW070543220526
45467CB00003B/1038